FEET OF CLAY

Terry Pratchett

FEET OF CLAY

adapted by Stephen Briggs

OBERON BOOKS
LONDON

WWW.OBERONBOOKS.COM

First published in 2015 by Oberon Books Ltd
521 Caledonian Road, London N7 9RH
Tel: +44 (0) 20 7607 3637 / Fax: +44 (0) 20 7607 3629
e-mail: info@oberonbooks.com
www.oberonbooks.com

A catalogue record for this book is available from the British
Library.

PB ISBN: 978-1-78319-195-6
E ISBN: 978-1-78319-694-4

Cover image by Paul Kidby
www.paulkidby.net

Visit www.oberonbooks.com to read more about all our books
and to buy them. You will also find features, author interviews and
news of any author events, and you can sign up for e-newsletters
so that you're always first to hear about our new releases.

Introduction

The first people *ever* to dramatise the Discworld, in any form, were the Studio Theatre Club in Abingdon, Oxon. That was in 1991, with *Wyrd Sisters*. We had already staged our own adaptations of other works: Monty Python's *Life of Brian* and *Holy Grail* – and Tom Sharpe's *Porterhouse Blue* and *Blott on the Landscape*. We were looking for something new when someone said 'Try Terry Pratchett – you'll like him'. So I ventured into the previously uncharted territory of the 'Fantasy' section of the local bookstore ('Here Be Dragons'). I read a Terry Pratchett book; I liked it. I read all of them. I wrote to Terry and asked if we could stage *Wyrd Sisters* . He said yes. *Wyrd Sisters* sold out. So did *Mort* the year after. So did *Guards! Guards!*, *Men at Arms, Maskerade, Jingo, Carpe Jugulum, The Fifth Elephant, The Truth, Night Watch, Interesting Times, Monstrous Regiment* and all the others in the years after that. In fact, 'sold out' is too modest a word. 'Oversold very quickly so that by the time the local newspaper mentioned it was on we'd had to close the booking office' is nearer the mark.

My casts were all happy enough to read whichever book we were staging, and to read others in the canon, too. The books stand on their own, but some knowledge of the wider Discworld ethos is essential when adapting the stories, and can also help Directors to find out where it's all coming from, and the actors with their characterisations.

The Discworld novels have been getting longer, more complex and darker as the years have passed and it is an increasing problem to try to put over the main plot while still meeting the over-riding target for amdram – getting into the pub before closing. The important thing is to decide what is the basic plot: anything which didn't contribute to that was liable to be dropped in order to keep the play flowing. Favourite scenes, even favourite characters, have on occasions had to be dumped. These are hard decisions but the book has to work as a *play*. You can't get 400 pages of novel into 2/2.5 hours on stage without sacrifices.

Each play also offers a challenge to Directors in working out who can double for whom in order to stage them with a smaller cast. You'll see from the cast list which follows this introduction how *we* covered all the roles.

Although the majority of our audiences are 'fans', I've tried to remember when writing the plays that not *all* the audience will be steeped in Discworld lore. Some of them may just be normal theatre-goers who'd never read a fantasy novel in their whole lives – humorous fantasy may not be their 'thing'. *Feet of Clay* is definitely a plot more suited to companies with a core of Discworld regulars in their audiences but even so, I wouldn't want 'newbies' to feel they were watching something which had been typed on an Enigma machine.

The books are episodic and have a sort of 'cinematic' construction; I have retained this format in *Feet of Clay* and used different stage areas and levels with brisk lighting changes to keep the action flowing. Set changes slow down the action, even when they're really slick. A thirty-second blackout between each scene, accompanied by rustling, crashing and muffled swearing from your stage crew means you're in danger of losing the audience. Even *ten*-second changes, if repeated often enough, will lead to loss of interest. I've been to see many productions of the plays and the best have been those that have used bare stages or composite sets – leaving the majority of the 'scene changing' to the lighting technician. The golden rule is – if you *can* do it without scene shifting, *do* it without scene shifting. It's a concept that has served radio drama very well (everyone *knows* that radio has the best scenery). And Shakespeare managed very well without it, too.

The plays do, however, call for some unusual props. Over the years, many of these have been made by my casts and crew: large hourglasses for Death's house, shadow puppets, archaic rifles, dragon-scorched books, and some matching candlesticks (one burned down, one fresh, one fresh and lit) for Vetinari's room in *Feet of Clay*. Other, more specialised props were put 'out to contract': Death's sword and scythe, an orang-utan, Detritus' head and hands, a Death of Rats, a Greebo, Scraps the dog and two swamp dragons (one an elaborate hand puppet and one with a fire-proof compartment in its bottom for a flight scene). Nowadays, I can't imagine how I cope without eBay.

Since the Studio Theatre Club started the trend in 1991, Terry and I have had many enquiries about staging the books – from as far afield as Finland, Zimbabwe, Indonesia, Australia, Bermuda and the Czech Republic (as well as Sheffield, Aberdeen, Exeter and the Isle of Man). I even licensed a production of *Wyrd Sisters* in Antarctica! Royalties from the five plays administered by *us* have raised over £90,000 so far for the Orangutan Foundation.

So how did our productions actually go? We enjoyed them. Our audiences seemed to enjoy them (after all, some of them were prepared, year after year, to travel down to Abingdon in Oxfordshire from Taunton, Newcastle-upon-Tyne, Ipswich, Basingstoke and…well, Oxford). Terry seems to enjoy them, too. He says that many of our members looked as though they had been recruited straight off the streets of Ankh-Morpork. He said that several of them were born to play the 'rude mechanicals' in Vitoller's troupe in *Wyrd Sisters.* He said that in his mind's eye the famous Ankh-Morpork City Watch *are* the players of the Studio Theatre Club.

I'm sure these were meant to be compliments.

By the time we staged *Feet of Clay* in 2007, we knew from long experience that the Discworld plays were a winner… though we'd also learned that the flourishing trade in other groups staging the plays meant that we couldn't afford to take full houses for granted. They're still full, but we do have to work a bit now to achieve that.

As with all the adaptations, there were difficult choices about which scenes should be sacrificed to try and keep the play down to a reasonable running time. We had also realised that Abingdon's medieval Unicorn Theatre was a part of the package; it has its shortcomings, but its ambience contributed much to the original success of the shows.

This dramatisation was written with the Unicorn Theatre's restrictions, and the number of players I expected to have available, in mind. Really complicated scenic effects were virtually impossible. Basically, we had a bare stage with an on-stage balcony at the back of the stage and a small curtained area beneath it. Anyone thinking of staging a Discworld play can be as imaginative as they like – call upon the might of Industrial Light & Magic, if it's within their budget. But *Feet of Clay can* be staged with only a relatively modest outlay on special effects. Bigger groups, with teams of experts on hand, can let their imaginations run wild!

In short, though, our experience and that of other groups is that it pays to work hard on getting the costumes and lighting right, and to keep the scenery to little more than, perhaps, a few changes of level enhanced by lighting effects and carefully chosen background music. There's room for all sorts of ideas here. The Discworld, as it says in the books, is your mollusc.

CHARACTERISATION

Within the constraints of what is known and vital about each character, there is still room for flexibility of interpretation. With the main roles, though, you have to recognise that your audiences will expect them to look as much like the book descriptions as possible. Most drama clubs don't have a vast range from which to choose, though, and it's the acting that's more important than the look of the player when it comes down to it.

COSTUMES

The City Watch 'style' is English Civil War. Vetinari wears a long, ecclesiastical-looking black robe and a black skull cap (or a black nightshirt when he's poorly). The rest of the city tends towards Dickensian.

SCENERY

Virtually none. On stage throughout was a desk and chair on one side of the stage, covered in clutter, to form the Watch office and a desk and chair on the other side with Vetinari's candle(s) and a writing slope, pen, etc., for the Palace. Apart from that, a virtually bare stage.

OH, AND A WORD ON PRONUNCIATION…

Having seen many of the plays staged, pronunciation of the names seems sometimes to be a stumbling block. Here are some pointers:

Ankh-Morpork	Ankh, as in 'bank', Morpork as in 'more pork', with the stress in the city's name on the second syllable – Ankh-<u>Mor</u>pork.
Vetinari	Long 'a' and stress the third syllable – Vetin<u>ah</u>-ri.
Angua	With a hard 'g' – 'An-Gwa' or 'An-Gewa', stress on the first syllable
Überwald	The 'U' as for German with an umlaut. So '<u>Eu</u>-ber-valt'.

THINKING OF STAGING IT..?

Application for professional performance etc. should be made before rehearsal to Colin Smythe Limited, 38 Mill Lane, Gerrards Cross, Bucks. SL9 8BA (CPSmythe@aol.com), and for amateur performance etc. to Oberon Books Ltd., 521 Caledonian Road, London N7 9RH (info@oberonbooks.com). No performance may be given unless a licence has been obtained.

Stephen Briggs,
September 2014
www.stephenbriggs.com

Terry Pratchett's *Feet Of Clay*, dramatised by Stephen Briggs was first presented by the Studio Theatre Club at the Unicorn Theatre, Abingdon, on Tuesday 23 January 2007, with the following cast and crew:

CMDR VIMES	Nigel Tait
CAPTAIN CARROT	Mark Pritchard
CPL NOBBY NOBBS	Graham Cook
SGT COLON	Anthony Walker
SGT DETRITUS	Jon Viner
CHEERY LITTLEBOTTOM	Sharon Preston
CONSTABLE VISIT	Alison Hodgkinson
CPL ANGUA	Kath Leighton
CONSTABLE DOWNSPOUT	Gaurav Kumar
DORFL	Lucy Potter
KING GOLEM	Gaurav Kumar
DRAGON KING OF ARMS	Matthew Kirk
PARDESSUS	Jamie Crowther
LORD VETINARI	Stephen Briggs
DRUMKNOTT	Sarah Hyland
MILDRED EASY	Farah Malik
DOUGHNUT JIMMY	Simon Cooper
MAID	Alix Palmer
ARTHUR CARRY	Andy Tatem
MR BOGGIS	John Conway
DR DOWNEY	Heather Neary
ROSIE PALM	Carolyne Harrison
QUEEN MOLLY	Vivienne Miles
GERHARDT SOCK	John Kirchhoff
SLANT	Helen Aston
FOOTMAN	Chris Turley
LADY SELACHI	Kat Parry
VENTURI	Laura Williams
RADDLEY	Ieuan James
PREBBLE SKINK	Briony Tatem
CANDLE MAKER	Sarah Hickingbottom
FR TUBELCEK	Patrice Meunier
Director	Stephen Briggs
Lighting/Effects	Colin James
Sound	Phil Evans
Stage Manager	Penny Hoile

ACT ONE

SCENE ONE

A bare stage. Thunder. Lightning. Dark, mysterious music. Curtains open to reveal the body of a priest (FATHER TUBELCEK). Centre back – SERGEANT COLON and CORPORAL NOBBS stand on patrol. Citizens move across the stage. A passer-by approaches a 'seamstress' in front of the watchmen, they exchange money, link arms and exit. In clear view another passer-by is accosted by a couple of thieves, hands over their cash and jewels and (having been given a receipt), go on their way. No reaction from the watchmen. A mime artist enters and starts to perform; a few people stop and watch. COLON and NOBBS move swiftly across and arrest him. LORD VETINARI and DRUMKNOTT enter. The WATCHMEN advise him of the arrest and he indicates the sentence. The MIME is shoved head first down the trapdoor and it is slammed down after him/her. The curtains close. VETINARI and DRUMKNOTT breeze out. COLON and NOBBY patrol off.

SGT. COLON: Quiet old night Nobby.

NOBBY NOBBS: Certainly is, Sarge.

> *COLON and NOBBS exit. A golem enters, with another golem (the KING GOLEM), and crosses to a door. He knocks. A man (MR CARRY) enters.*

ARTHUR CARRY: Well? What do you want at this time of night?

> *The golem hands him a slate. He reads, then answers…*

Yes, I am Arthur Carry, the candle maker.

> *He reads on.*

'We Hear You Want A Golem'? Hah. *Want,* yes. *Afford,* no.

> *The golem rubs the words off the slate and writes. The man reads.*

'To You, One Hundred Dollars'. For you? You're the one that's for sale?

The golem shakes his head. Another, white, golem enters.

A hundred dollars? What's wrong with it?

The golem writes again.

'Ninety Dollars.' *(Pause.)* 'Eighty Dollars.' It looks…new. But no one's making golems any more…are they? Sounds like someone wants to get rid of it in a hurry…

More writing.

'Sixty Dollars'. The priests banned making 'em years ago.

More writing.

'Thirty Dollars'.

The man hands over some coins.

Done!

The white golem and man go into the house. The other golem exits slowly. VIMES saunters on and is intercepted by SGT COLON, who carries a clipboard.

SGT. COLON: Commander Vimes, sir! Bin a bit of an odd murder, sir. Down in one of them old houses on Misbegot Bridge. Some old priest. Father Tubelcek. Waiting for more details, sir.

COMMANDER VIMES: Right, Sergeant. Start looking into it. Anything else?

SGT. COLON: Corporal Nobbs is sick, sir.

COMMANDER VIMES: Well, everyone knows that, Fred.

SGT. COLON: I mean *off* sick, sir.

COMMANDER VIMES: Granny's funeral again?

SGT. COLON: Nossir.

COMMANDER VIMES: How many's he had this year…?

SGT. COLON: Seven, sir.

COMMANDER VIMES: Very odd family, the Nobbses. You and Mrs Colon looking forward to retirement, Fred?

SGT. COLON: *(Very unconvincing.)* Can't wait sir. All that fresh air. Exercise. Up to my armpit in livestock…

COMMANDER VIMES: Quite. Anything else?

SGT. COLON: Applicant for that alchemy job.

He calls, off.

In here.

CHEERY enters.

COMMANDER VIMES: So. You're an alchemist.

CHEERY LITTLEBOTTOM: That's right, sir.

COMMANDER VIMES: Guild member?

CHEERY LITTLEBOTTOM: Not any more, sir.

COMMANDER VIMES: Oh? How did you leave the guild?

CHEERY LITTLEBOTTOM: Through the roof, sir.

COMMANDER VIMES: Ah, the usual way, eh? What's your name, lad?

CHEERY LITTLEBOTTOM: *(With a sigh.)* Littlebottom, sir.

COMMANDER VIMES: *(No reaction.)* That means you're from the Überwald mountain area, yes?

CHEERY nods.

Our Constable Angua comes from there. And your first name…?

CHEERY LITTLEBOTTOM: Cheery, sir.

COMMANDER VIMES: *(Again, no reaction.)* Cheery, eh? Good to see the old naming traditions kept up. Cheery Littlebottom. Fine.

CHEERY LITTLEBOTTOM: *(Like one niggling at a scab.)* Yes, sir. Cheery Littlebottom. My father was Jolly. Jolly Littlebottom.

COMMANDER VIMES: *(Stone-faced.)* Really?

CHEERY LITTLEBOTTOM: And *his* father was Beaky Littlebottom.

COMMANDER VIMES: Know anything about dead bodies?

CHEERY LITTLEBOTTOM: Yes, sir!

COMMANDER VIMES: Good. Listen. I know about how to be a copper. But there's lots of things I don't know. You fellows know how to mix things up in bowls and can find out all sorts of stuff. Maybe the dead person was poisoned? We need someone who knows what colour a liver is supposed to be. I want someone who can look at the ashtray and tell me what kind of cigars I smoke.

CHEERY LITTLEBOTTOM: Pantweed's Slim Panatellas. The packet's in your pocket, sir.

COMMANDER VIMES: OK. I expect you to work to the job not the clock. We're just one big family and, when you've been to a few domestic disputes, Littlebottom, I can assure you that you'll see the resemblance. Technically you'll rank as a corporal, only don't go giving orders to real policemen. You're on a month's trial. Now, find an iconograph and meet me on Misbegot Bridge in…damn… better make it an hour. I've got to see about this blasted coat of arms. Sergeant Detritus!

DETRITUS enters.

DETRITUS: Sir?

COMMANDER VIMES: This is Corporal Littlebottom. Corporal Cheery Littlebottom, whose father was Jolly Littlebottom. Give him his badge, swear him in, show him where everything is.

Well, off you go, Littlebottom. Detritus will look after you.

CHEERY LITTLEBOTTOM: Sir. Um…were you going to say 'You can make it *big* in the Watch', sir?

COMMANDER VIMES: No. Why?

CHEERY LITTLEBOTTOM: Er… I *did* tell you my name, didn't I, sir?

COMMANDER VIMES: Yes. Cheery Littlebottom. Yes?

CHEERY LITTLEBOTTOM: Er…yes. That's right. Well, thank you, sir.

CHEERY & DETRITUS leave. A moment, then…

COMMANDER VIMES: *(Ramming his fist into his mouth to muffle the laughter.)* 'Cheery Littlebottom!'

Blackout. Lights up on FATHER TUBELCEK's body. CARROT and VISIT stand by the 'body', with MRS KANACKI.

CARROT: And this is how you found him, ma'am?

MRS KANACKI: Yes. I brought him his breakfast like always, and this is how he was.

CARROT: *Just* like this, ma'am?

MRS KANACKI: Yes. That's right. Who'd want to…he was a lovely man. Lovely.

CARROT: *(To VISIT.)* What's that in his mouth, Constable Visit? A cigarette?

VISIT: *(Taking it.)* No, Captain. It's a rolled-up note.

Opening it.

It's an ancient Klatchian script. One of the desert tribes called the Cenotines, sir.

CARROT: Do you know what it means?

VISIT: I could find out, sir.

CARROT: Good. Mr Vimes will want to know.

He looks down at the floor by the body.

The old man is viciously attacked. Then someone – maybe it was him, dying, maybe it was the murderer – writes something down and rolls it up neatly and pops it into his mouth like a condemned man's cigarette. Then he does die and someone shuts his eyes and…does what? Walks out into the seething hurly-burly that is Ankh-Morpork? What's this?

VISIT: *(Looking.)* Dirt. You get it on floors. Specially this near the river.

CARROT: Except this is off-white. We're on black loam.

VISIT: Ah. A Clue. There's some on the windowsill, too. Maybe there are footprints outside…

He wanders off to one side.

CARROT: There's a thirty-foot drop into the river outside the window. There won't be any footprints – I mean, even on a river as thick as the Ankh any footprints'd be bound to have oozed back by now.

He looks at the floor and picks up some of the white dirt.

White clay. Where the hell is white clay around here?

Blackout.

SCENE TWO

The College of Heralds. Noise, off, of a variety of odd animals. We hear PARDESSUS CHATAIN PURSUIVANT. A doorbell clangs, off.

PARDESSUS: *(Off.)* Down, boy! Couchant! I said couchant! No! *Not* rampant! And thee shall have a sugar lump like a good boy. William! Stop that at once! Put him down! Mildred, let go of Graham!

He enters, looking very flustered and crosses to the other door. VIMES enters.

COMMANDER VIMES: Commander Vimes. I have an appointment.

PARDESSUS: Oh. I suppose thee'd better come in.

More animal noises, off.

COMMANDER VIMES: Ye gods! What's that?

PARDESSUS: Those are the heraldic beasts.

Blank look from VIMES.

For the coats of arms?

COMMANDER VIMES: I just thought you made them up. What – you paint them from life then?

PARDESSUS: Of course. Make them up indeed! Mind you, we could do with a female hippo. I mean, it's just not natural for Roderick and Keith, I ain't passing judgement, it's just not right, that's all I'm saying. What was thy name again?

COMMANDER VIMES: Vimes. Sir Samuel Vimes.

DRAGON KING OF ARMS enters.

DRAGON KING OF ARMS: Ah, Sir Samuel. Welcome. Dragon King of Arms.

VIMES' hand moves to his sword.

You will not need your sword, Commander. I have been Dragon King of Arms for more than five hundred years but I do not breathe fire, I assure you. Ah-ha. Ah-ha.

COMMANDER VIMES: Ah-ha. Five hundred years? Ah – you're a bloody vampire.

DRAGON KING OF ARMS: Quite so. Thank you Pardessus. You may go about your duties.

PARDESSUS leaves.

Yes. Vampire, indeed. Yes, I've heard about your views on vampires. 'Not really alive but not dead enough,' I believe you have said. I think that is rather clever. Ah-ha. Vampire, yes. *Bloody*, no.

(He shows his black ribboner badge.) League of Temperence, see? I'm afraid your time has been needlessly wasted, Commander Vimes.

COMMANDER VIMES: I don't understand.

DRAGON KING OF ARMS: I believe you're here because it is considered, ah-ha, appropriate that you have a coat of arms. I am afraid that this is not possible. Ah-ha. A Vimes coat of arms *has* existed, but it cannot be resurrected. It would be against the rules.

COMMANDER VIMES: What rules?

DRAGON KING OF ARMS: I'm sure you know your ancestry, Commander.

COMMANDER VIMES: It's Old Stoneface, isn't it.

DRAGON KING OF ARMS: Indeed. Ah-ha. Suffer-Not-Injustice Vimes. Your ancestor. Old Stoneface, indeed, as he was called. Commander of the City Watch in 1688. And a regicide. He murdered the last king of Ankh-Morpork, as every schoolboy knows.

COMMANDER VIMES: Executed!

DRAGON KING OF ARMS: Nevertheless, the family crest was, as we say in heraldry, *Depositatum De Latrina*. Destroyed. Banned.

COMMANDER VIMES: Are you telling me I *can't* have a coat of arms?

DRAGON KING OF ARMS: This is so.

COMMANDER VIMES: Because my ancestor killed a –

DRAGON KING OF ARMS: He was the king.

COMMANDER VIMES: Oh, yes. And he was fond of children. *Very* fond of children. And in the dungeons he had machines for –

DRAGON KING OF ARMS: Commander. I feel you do not understand me. *Whatever else he was,* he was the king. You see, a crown is not like a Watchman's helmet. Even when you take it off, it's still on the head. There is seldom a reward for those who do what must be done. But, still… I was extremely pleased, Commander, to hear of your marriage to Lady Sybil. An excellent lineage. One of the most noble families in the city, ah-ha. The Ramkins, the Selachiis, the Nobbses, the Venturis, of course… Once we dealt with *real* heraldry. But this, they tell me, is the Century of the Fruitbat. Now it seems that, as soon as a man opens his second meat-pie shop, he feels impelled to consider himself a gentleman. The butcher, the baker and the candlestick-maker. Well, the candlemaker, in point of fact. Pardessus!

PARDESSUS enters with a pad with heraldic devices.

COMMANDER VIMES: Isn't that one the Assassins' Guild?

DRAGON KING OF ARMS: No. Very like it though. Well
spotted. Mr Arthur Carry the candlemaker, in fact.
A shield bisected by a bend sinister d'une meche en
metal gris – that is to say, a steel grey shield indicating
his personal determination and zeal bisected by a wick.
Upper half, a chandelle in a fenêtre avec rideaux houlant
(a candle lighting a window), lower half two chandeliers
illumine (indicating he sells candles to rich and poor alike).
Fortunately his father was a harbourmaster, which fact
allowed us to *stretch* ourselves a little with a crest of a lampe
au poisson (fish-shaped lamp), indicating both his and his
son's current profession. The motto I left in the common
modern tongue and is 'Art Brought Forth the Candle'. Art,
Arthur? I'm sorry, it was naughty but I couldn't resist it.

COMMANDER VIMES: My sides ache.

DRAGON KING OF ARMS: While this one, is for Rudolph Potts
of the Bakers' Guild. Can you read it, Commander?

COMMANDER VIMES: Well, there's a rose, a flame and a pot.
Er…bakers use fire and the pot's for water, I suppose…

DRAGON KING OF ARMS: *And* a pun on the name.

COMMANDER VIMES: Hilarious. But, unless he's called Rosie,
I…oh Gods… A rose is a *flower*, right? Flower, flour. Flour,
fire and water? The pot looks like a guzunder to me,
though. A chamber pot?

DRAGON KING OF ARMS: The old word for baker was *pistor*.
Why, Commander, we shall make a Herald of you yet!
And the motto?

COMMANDER VIMES: *'Quod Subigo Farinam,'* 'Because'…
'farinaceous' means to do with corn, or flour, doesn't it? …
oh, no… 'Because I Knead the Dough'?

DRAGON KING OF ARMS: Well done, sir!

COMMANDER VIMES: This place must simply rock on those long winter evenings. And that's heraldry, is it? Crossword clues and plays on words?

Hold on – you said 'Nobbs'! Before – when you were talking about old families! You don't mean Nobbs as in… Corporal Nobbs?

DRAGON KING OF ARMS: Would that be a C. W. St J. Nobbs?

COMMANDER VIMES: Er… yes. Yes!

DRAGON KING OF ARMS: Grandson of Slope Nobbs, who was the illegitimate son of Edward St John de Nobbes, Earl of Ankh, and a, ah-ha, a parlourmaid of unknown lineage. You know the gentleman?

VIMES nods, stunned. The doorbell rings; PARDESSUS exits.

Excellent! I thought that he was the one. Is he a man of property?

COMMANDER VIMES: Only other people's.

DRAGON KING OF ARMS: Well, do tell him. There is no land or money now, of course, but the title is still extant.

COMMANDER VIMES: Corporal Nobbs…my Corporal Nobbs…is *the Earl of Ankh?*

DRAGON KING OF ARMS: Yes, it would appear so.

COMMANDER VIMES: Nobby? Good gods!

DRAGON KING OF ARMS: Well, well! This has been a *very* happy meeting.

PARDESSUS re-enters with SGT COLON in tow.

SGT. COLON: Sir! You're needed at the Patrician's Palace, sir!

COMMANDER VIMES: Yes, I know Fred. Appointment at…

SGT. COLON: Nossir. This is urgent.

With a nod to DRAGON KING OF ARMS, VIMES & COLON leave.

PARDESSUS: So that was Commander Sir Samuel Vimes.

DRAGON KING OF ARMS: Stupid man. And people like that rise to high office these days.

Ah – you have completed the design?

PARDESSUS: All according to your instructions, sir.

He opens the pad at the right page.

DRAGON KING OF ARMS: *(Reading.)* 'The Descent of King Carrot I, by the Grace of the Gods King of Ankh-Morpork'. 'Married... Delphine Angua von Überwald.'

He chuckles.

I am very pleased with her lineage, Pardessus. Quite an achievement, but werewolves take quite a lot of interest in...pedigree.

PARDESSUS: Queen of Ankh? But they're *not* married. And that can't happen, sir. She's a...

DRAGON KING OF ARMS: Species is a secondary consideration. What really matters in an individual was a good pedigree. Ah, well. This is the future as it *might* be.

But we need another candidate to put to the Guild leaders, Pardessus.

PARDESSUS: But surely it should be the rightful king...?

DRAGON KING OF ARMS: People talk about the true king of Ankh-Morpork, but the *true* king is the one who gets crowned.

Lights out.

SCENE THREE

Dwarf Bread Museum. MR HOPKINSON lies dead. VISIT stands upstage, guarding the scene. CARROT and ANGUA enter from the back room.

CARROT: Anything?

ANGUA: I can smell him, and you, and the bread, and that's it.

CARROT: Nothing else?

ANGUA: Dirt. Dust. The usual stuff. Oh, there are some old traces, days old. I know you were in here last week, for example. There are lots of smells. Grease, meat, pine resin for some reason, old food…but I'll swear no living thing's been in here in the last day or so but him and us.

CARROT: But you told me everyone leaves a trail. What about a vampire..?

ANGUA: Carrot, I could tell if a vampire had been in here in the last *month*.

CARROT: There's almost half a dollar in pennies in the cash drawer. Anyway, a thief would be here for the valuable Battle Bread, wouldn't they?

ANGUA gives him a cynical look.

It is a very valuable cultural artefact.

I come in once a month just to have a chat. He lets me handle the exhibits, you know.

ANGUA: That must be fun.

She wanders off.

CARROT: *(Wistfully.)* Yes. Yes it is.

ANGUA: *(Off.)* This is quite an oven.

CARROT: He researches old recipes. He does special orders. Replica throwing scones, close-combat crumpets and so on – for wealthy dwarfs here in the city. It's quite an art.

ANGUA: *(Re-entering.)* There *is* something else. Faint. Not a living thing. Something like dirt, but not quite. It's kind of… yellow-orange…

CARROT: *(Tactfully.)* Er… Some of us don't have your special, werewolf sense of smell…

ANGUA: I've smelled it before, somewhere in this town. Can't remember where… It's strong. Stronger than the other smells. It's a muddy smell. No, not mud. Sharper. More treble.

They start to walk out of the scene and cross the stage to exit.

CARROT: You know, sometimes I envy you. It must be nice to be a wolf. Just for a while.

ANGUA: It has its drawbacks. Fleas. The constant nagging feeling that you should be wearing three bras at once. You learn to keep it under control. OK, there is the occasional chicken, but I always go round next day to shove some money under the door.

CARROT: Well, that's…

ANGUA: It's very hard being a vegetarian who has to pick bits of meat out of their teeth in the morning. It's easy to be a vegetarian by day. It's stopping yourself from becoming a *humani*tarian at night that takes the effort.

She, followed by CARROT, exit as the lights blackout.

SCENE FOUR

The Patrician's Palace. DRUMKNOTT hurries on, followed by VIMES. LORD VETINARI is slumped in his chair, looking very unwell.

DRUMKNOTT: Commander! Thank goodness you've come! It's his lordship…

VIMES crosses to VETINARI.

LORD VETINARI: Ah… Commander Vimes…

COMMANDER VIMES: What's been happening, sir?

LORD VETINARI: I appear to be slightly unwell, Vimes.

COMMANDER VIMES: Drumknott says you were unconscious this morning, sir.

LORD VETINARI: Dear me. I must have been…overdoing it. Well, thank you. If you would be kind enough to…help me up…

He starts to rise, then flops back into the chair. COLON enters to VIMES.

COMMANDER VIMES: Ah, Fred. Who've you got down there so far?

SGT. COLON: There's me and Constable Flint and Constable Slapper, sir.

COMMANDER VIMES: Right. Someone's to go up to my place and get Willikins to bring me my sword and crossbow. And an overnight bag. And some cigars. And tell Lady Sybil…tell Lady Sybil…well, they'll just have to tell Lady Sybil I've got to deal with things down here, that's all.

SGT. COLON: What's *happening*, sir? Someone downstairs said Lord Vetinari's dead!

LORD VETINARI: Dead? Nonsense!

He pulls himself to his feet, then collapses gently to the floor.

COMMANDER VIMES: *(As he and COLON help VETINARI back onto his chair.)* His lordship's just a bit… I reckon he's been poisoned, Fred, and that's the truth of it.

SGT. COLON: Do you want me to get a doctor?

COMMANDER VIMES: Are you mad? We want him to live! *(Pause.)* But someone ought to look at him… Send a runner up to the stables on Kings Down to fetch Doughnut Jimmy.

SGT. COLON: Doughnut? He doesn't know anything about doctoring! He dopes racehorses!

COMMANDER VIMES: Just get him, Fred. There's going to be a lot of people turning up pretty soon. I want a couple of Watchmen outside this room and no one is to come in without my permission, right?

SGT. COLON: But…*poisoned?* He's got food-tasters and everything!

COMMANDER VIMES: Then maybe it was one of them, Fred.

SGT. COLON: My gods, sir! You don't trust *anyone*, do you?

COMMANDER VIMES: No, Fred. Incidentally, was it you? Just kidding. Off you go. We don't have much time.

COLON exits. VIMES turns to the semi-conscious VETINARI.

Poison. That's the worst of all. It doesn't make a noise, the poisoner can be miles away, you can't see it, often you can't really smell it or taste it, it could be anywhere – and there it is, doing its work…

LORD VETINARI: I would like a glass of water.

COMMANDER VIMES: *(Reaches for the jug on the desk, then hesitates.)* I'll send someone to get some.

LORD VETINARI: Ah, Sir Samuel…but whom can you trust?

Blackout.

SCENE FIVE

MRS KANACKI's. FATHER TUBELCEK's body is on. CHEERY is examining it. DETRITUS stands to one side. CHEERY is rootling under the corpse's fingernails and examining the result with a magnifying glass.

CHEERY LITTLEBOTTOM: He's been hit repeatedly around the head. Some kind of very heavy blunt instrument. No other obvious signs of violence, although…

Examining the nail scrapings.

Something piled under the nails. Waxy, like thick grease.

CHEERY takes an envelope out of his pocket and scrapes the stuff into it, seals it up and numbers it. CHEERY then takes up the iconograph and photographs TUBELCEK's eyes.

DETRITUS: Why you take picture of his eyes?

CHEERY LITTLEBOTTOM: They do say the last thing you see remains imprinted on your eyes. I thought I could see two red glowing dots when I looked in there. I can enlarge the image and check what's there.

WENGEL RADDLEY enters.

DETRITUS: Yes?

WENGEL RADDLEY: I am Wengel Raddley and I am a person of some standing in this community and I demand that you let us have poor Father Tubelcek this minute!

DETRITUS: We're, er, we're trying to find out who killed him.

WENGEL RADDLEY: But we want to take Father Tubelcek away to bury him.

DETRITUS: *(To CHEERY.)* You done everyfing you need?

CHEERY LITTLEBOTTOM: I suppose so…

DETRITUS: He dead?

CHEERY LITTLEBOTTOM: Oh, yes.

DETRITUS: He gonna get any better?

CHEERY LITTLEBOTTOM: Er…no.

DETRITUS: *(To RADDLEY.)* Okay, den you people can take him away.

A WATCHMAN calls from below.

WATCHMAN: *(Off.)* Is there someone up there called… *(With a barely suppressed snigger.)* … 'Cheery Littlebottom?'

CHEERY LITTLEBOTTOM: Yes.

WATCHMAN *(Off.)* Well, Commander Vimes says you've to come to the Patrician's palace right now, all right?

DETRITUS: And Dat's *Corporal* Little Bottom!

Blackout.

SCENE SIX

The Patrician's Palace. On stage are representatives of the City's Guilds – MR BOGGIS (Thieves), LORD DOWNEY (Assassins), ROSIE PALM (Seamstresses), QUEEN MOLLY (Beggars), SLANT (Lawyers), etc. VIMES enters, with DRUMKNOTT. BOGGIS breaks away from the other Guild leaders and crosses to VIMES.

BOGGIS: What's going on, Vimes?

COMMANDER VIMES: I believe Lord Vetinari has been poisoned, Mr Boggis.

The background muttering stops and all eyes turn to VIMES.

BOGGIS: Er…fatally?

COMMANDER VIMES: Not yet.

DOWNEY: The Guild of Assassins has no contract for Lord Vetinari. Besides, as I am sure is common knowledge, we have set the price for the Patrician at one million dollars.

COMMANDER VIMES: And who has that sort of money, indeed?

DOWNEY: Well…you for one, Sir Samuel.

Nervous laughter.

BOGGIS: We wish to see Lord Vetinari, in any case.

COMMANDER VIMES: No. Doctor's orders.

BOGGIS: Really? Which doctor?

COMMANDER VIMES: Dr James Folsom.

BOGGIS: What? You can't mean… Doughnut Jimmy? He's a *horse* doctor! But why?

COMMANDER VIMES: Because many of *his* patients survive. And now, gentlemen, if you will excuse us. Somewhere there's a poisoner. I'd like to find him before he becomes a murderer.

The Guild leaders file out as the scene changes to LORD VETINARI's chair, where he sits with a blanket over his legs and a cushion behind his head. CHEERY is on with DOUGHNUT JIMMY.

Cheery? What have you discovered?

CHEERY LITTLEBOTTOM: You were right, sir. It *could* be arsenic poisoning.

COMMANDER VIMES: Jimmy – thanks for coming. Arsenic, eh?

DOUGHNUT JIMMY: Nasty stuff. Has he been eating his bedding?

CHEERY LITTLEBOTTOM: *(A little confused.)* All the sheets seemed to be here, so I suppose the answer is no.

DOUGHNUT JIMMY: How's he pissing?

CHEERY LITTLEBOTTOM: *(Embarrassed.)* Er. The usual way, I assume.

DOUGHNUT JIMMY: Walk him round a bit on the loose rein.

LORD VETINARI: You *are* a doctor, are you?

DOUGHNUT JIMMY: Well, er... I have a lot of patients.

LORD VETINARI: Indeed? I have very little.

DOUGHNUT JIMMY: *(Moving away from VETINARI. VIMES and CHEERY follow.)* I'll mix up a draught. You're to hold his nose and pour it down his throat twice a day, right? And no oats.

COMMANDER VIMES: I'm sure it won't be the food-tasters. For all they know they might be asked to eat the whole plateful. You find out the *how,* right? And then leave the *who* to me.

VIMES and JIMMY leave. CHEERY moves back to VETINARI.

CHEERY LITTLEBOTTOM: *(To herself.)* If you didn't eat or drink a poison, what else is there? Put it on a pad and hold it on their face? Dribble some in their ear while they sleep? Or they could touch it. Maybe a small dart... Or an insect bite...

LORD VETINARI: Tell me, young man, are you a policeman?

CHEERY LITTLEBOTTOM: Er...just started, sir.

LORD VETINARI: You appear to be of the dwarf persuasion.

(He talks to himself.) Arsenic is a very popular poison. Hundreds of uses around the home. And used for dyeing fabrics and wallpapers... Crushed diamonds used to be in vogue for hundreds of years, despite the fact they never worked. Mercury is for those with patience, aquafortis for those without. But we return to arsenic like an old, old friend. Is that not so, young Vetinari? Yes indeed, sir. But where then shall we put it, seeing that all will look for it? In the last place they will look, sir. Wrong. We put it where no one will *look.....*

CHEERY LITTLEBOTTOM: Cloth dye? Bed linen… wallpaper….

She calls, off.

In here!

DRUMKNOTT enters.

Get another bed. From anywhere. And fresh bed linen. And let's get rid of this green wallpaper, too!!

DRUMKNOTT hurries off. DETRITUS ambles across, carrying a battered chair.

DETRITUS: Dis will have to do.

CHEERY LITTLEBOTTOM: What? Detritus, what are you doing?

DETRITUS: I can easily break off der back. Ole Doughnut said for to get a stool sample.

Blackout.

SCENE SEVEN

The Watch House. VIMES and COLON are on stage.

SGT COLON: We checked the food tasters, sir. No problems.

COMMANDER VIMES: Well no. Vetinari chose them himself. The tasters are well paid and treated.

SGT. COLON: And they're the sons of the chief cook.

COMMANDER VIMES: His main protection is that he's more useful alive than dead, from everyone's point of view. The big powerful guilds don't like him, but they like him in power a lot more than they liked the idea of someone from a rival guild in the Oblong Office. Besides, he represents stability.

SGT COLON: Sir?

COMMANDER VIMES: He told me that himself once. 'People think they want good government and justice for all,

Vimes, yet what is it they really crave? Only that things go on as normal and tomorrow is pretty much like today.' Trouble is, he's right. What's my next move, Fred?

SGT COLON: Dunno, sir.

COMMANDER VIMES: No one's in charge, that's the problem.

SGT COLON: Could be, sir. There again, you never know your luck.

He winks, knowingly.

COMMANDER VIMES: Listen, Fred, if there *is* to be a new ruler, it won't be me…. Hang on. You don't mean me, do you. You mean Carrot.

SGT COLON: Could be, sir. I mean none of the guilds'd let some other guild bloke be ruler now, and everyone likes Captain Carrot, and, well…rumour's got about that he's the hair to the throne, sir.

COMMANDER VIMES: There's no proof of that, Sergeant.

SGT COLON: He's got that sword of his, and the birthmark shaped like a crown, and…well , everyone *knows* he's king. It's his krisma.

COMMANDER VIMES: No more kings, Fred.

SGT COLON: Right you are, sir. By the way, Nobby's turned up. You said you'd talk to him about all these funerals, sir…

COMMANDER VIMES: The day gets worse and worse. All right, go and tell him to come up here.

COLON goes to the door and nods to NOBBY (off), who then enters as COLON leaves.

Come in, Nobby.

NOBBY NOBBS: Er, Fred said you wanted to see me, Mr Vimes, on account of timekeeping…

COMMANDER VIMES: Did I? Did I? Oh, yes. Nobby, how many grandmothers' funerals have you *really* been to?

NOBBY NOBBS: Er…three…

COMMANDER VIMES: Three?

NOBBY NOBBS: It turned out Nanny Nobbs weren't quite dead the first time.

COMMANDER VIMES: There's something else I've got to tell you, Nobby. Do you remember your father?

NOBBY NOBBS: Old Sconner, sir? Not much, sir. Never used to see him much except when the milit'ry police used to come for to drag him outa the attic.

COMMANDER VIMES: Do you know much about your, er, antecedents?

NOBBY NOBBS: That is a lie, sir. I haven't got no antecedents, sir, no matter what you might have been tole.

COMMANDER VIMES: You don't actually know what 'antecedents' means, do you, Nobby?

NOBBY NOBBS: Not in so many words, sir.

COMMANDER VIMES: You never got told anything about your ancestors? Your Dad never left you anything?

NOBBY NOBBS: Coupla scars, sir. And this trick elbow of mine. And this, o' course…

NOBBY fishes around behind his rusting breastplate and pulls out a leather thong with a gold ring on it.

He left it to me when he was on his deathbed. Well, when I say 'left it'…

COMMANDER VIMES: Did he say anything?

NOBBY NOBBS: Well, yeah, he did say 'Give it back, you little bugger!', sir. See, 'e 'ad it on a string round his neck, sir, just like me. But it's not like a proper ring, sir. I'd have flogged it but it's all I got to remember him by.

COMMANDER VIMES: It's got a coat of arms on it. *(He sighs.)* When you've got a moment, nip along to the College of Heralds in Mollymog Street, will you? Take this ring with you and say I sent you.

NOBBY NOBBS: Er…

COMMANDER VIMES: It's all right. Nobby. You won't get into trouble. Off you go, then.

NOBBY salutes and exits. VIMES looks at the book he's been holding (Twurp's Peerage).

Reading.

'de Nobbes' There's even a damn coat of arms. He gets one; I don't. *(He sighs.)* Who has a motive for poisoning Vetinari? No, that's not the way. Of course, there is one person who stands to gain by his death. It's *me*, isn't it?

A knock at the door. CHEERY enters.

Yes, Littlebottom? How is his lordship?

CHEERY LITTLEBOTTOM: Stable.

COMMANDER VIMES: *Dead* is stable.

CHEERY LITTLEBOTTOM: I mean he's alive, sir, and sitting up reading. Mr Doughnut made up some sticky stuff that tasted of seaweed, sir. Sir, you know the old man in the house on the bridge? Er…have you ever heard the story about dead men's eyes, sir?

COMMANDER VIMES: Assume I haven't had a literary education, Littlebottom.

CHEERY LITTLEBOTTOM: Well… They say that the last thing a dying man sees stays imprinted in his eyes, sir.

I checked sir. Two glowing red eyes.

COMMANDER VIMES: Really? I just hope it's not a god of some sort.

CARROT and ANGUA enter.

CARROT: We found a murder, sir! At the Dwarf Bread Museum. But when we got back to the Watch House they told us Lord Vetinari's dead!

COMMANDER VIMES: He's breathing well for a corpse. I think he'll be okay for now.

CARROT: It'd be terrible for the city if anything happened to him!

COMMANDER VIMES: You mentioned another murder?

CARROT: At the Dwarf Bread Museum. Someone killed Mr Hopkinson with his own bread!

COMMANDER VIMES: Made him eat it?

CARROT: Hit him with it, sir. Battle Bread, sir. Angua *(CARROT taps his nose conspiratorially.)* couldn't find a sniff of anyone. And nothing was taken.

COMMANDER VIMES: Father Tubelcek and Mr Hopkinson. Why has someone killed two harmless old men. We shall find out. Constable Angua, I want you to have a look at this one. Take…yes, take Corporal Littlebottom. He's been doing some work on it. Angua's from Überwald too, Littlebottom. Maybe you've got friends in common, that sort of thing.

ANGUA/CHEERY: *(Both a bit doubtful.)* Yes, sir.

They both exit, as they go, ANGUA says.

ANGUA: Fancy a drink?

CARROT: What about Lord Vetinari?

COMMANDER VIMES: I'm putting my best man on that. Trustworthy, reliable, knows the ins and outs of this place like the back of his hand.

CARROT looks blank.

I'm handling it, in other words.

No. Not you. If anything happens to Vetinari, I don't want anyone to say you were anywhere near him, OK?

I want you to go back to the Watch House and take care of things. Rise to the occasion. Move paper around. There's that new shift rota to draw up. Shout at people! Read reports!

CARROT: Yes, Commander Vimes.

COMMANDER VIMES: Good. Off you go, then.

Lights out as CARROT exits.

SCENE EIGHT

Outside the College of Heralds. Animal noises, off. NOBBY walks up and knocks on the door. PARDESSUS enters.

PARDESSUS: Yes? What dost *thee* want?

NOBBY NOBBS: I'm Corporal Nobbs.

PARDESSUS: Are you the baboon? We've had one on order for…

NOBBY NOBBS: No. I've come about some coat with arms.

PARDESSUS: You?

NOBBY NOBBS: Commander Vimes sent me. It's about this ring I got.

PARDESSUS: Go round the back door.

Blackout.

SCENE NINE

A bar. ANGUA and CHEERY are sat, with ANGUA staring pointedly at CHEERY, who is looking a bit nervous. A bar…person enters. They look like an extra from a Hammer Horror film. CHEERY has an envelope (clay sample) on the table in front of her.

CHEERY LITTLEBOTTOM: What is this place?

ANGUA: It's…a place where people can be – themselves. People who…have to be a little careful at other times. You know?

CHEERY LITTLEBOTTOM: No.

ANGUA: Vampires, zombies, bogeymen, The und – The differently alive. People who have to spend most of their time being very careful, not frightening people, fitting in.

Sometimes it's good to go where everybody knows your shape.

CHEERY LITTLEBOTTOM: *(Indicating off.)* Who's that girl? She looks…normal .

ANGUA: That's Violet. She's a tooth fairy.

CHEERY LITTLEBOTTOM: Er…any werewolves here?

ANGUA: One or two. Actually…

CHEERY LITTLEBOTTOM: I hate werewolves. Oh, people say they can be tamed but I say, once a wolf, always a wolf. You can't trust them. They're basically evil, aren't they? They could go back to the wild at any moment, I say.

ANGUA: Yes. You may be right.

CHEERY LITTLEBOTTOM: And the worst thing is, most of the time they walk around looking just like real people.

ANGUA: Oh?

ANGUA stares at CHEERY.

CHEERY LITTLEBOTTOM: What?

ANGUA: Nothing. I just thought I'd say: don't worry, I won't tell anyone if you don't want me to.

CHEERY LITTLEBOTTOM: I don't know what you're talking about!

Pause.

How could you tell?

ANGUA: Shall we just say… I have special talents?

I don't know why you're so upset. I thought dwarfs hardly recognized the difference between male and female, anyway. Look, there's plenty of women in this town that'd love to do things the dwarf way. I mean, what're the choices they've got? Barmaid, seamstress or someone's wife. While *you* can do anything the men do…

CHEERY LITTLEBOTTOM: Provided we do *only* what the men do.

ANGUA: Oh. I *see*. Yes. I know *that* tune.

CHEERY LITTLEBOTTOM: I can't even drink dwarfishly! When I try to quaff I drown the dwarf behind me! I saw a girl walk down the street here and some men *whistled* after her! And you can wear *dresses!*

ANGUA: How long have lady dwarfs felt like this? I thought they were happy with the way things are…

CHEERY LITTLEBOTTOM: Oh, it's easy to be happy when you don't know any different!

I thought I could come to Ankh-Morpork and get a different kind of job.

ANGUA: I think you'll like it here. Everyone's got troubles in the Watch. Normal people don't become policemen. You'll get on fine.

CHEERY LITTLEBOTTOM: *You're* normal. I like *you.*

ANGUA: When you've been around here for a while you'll find out that sometimes I can be a bitch. *(Seeing the envelope.)*

What's that?

She picks it up, opens it and sniffs the contents.

CHEERY LITTLEBOTTOM: It's just clay. It was on the floor in the room where the old priest was killed. I think it's just potters' clay. This looks like someone tried baking it but didn't get the heat right. See how it crumbles?

I showed it to Igneous the Troll – he runs the pottery warehouse?

ANGUA: Yes, I know Igneous.

CHEERY LITTLEBOTTOM: He told me…

She takes out her notebook and reads.

''Dis is crank. Dat's like…crappy clay, jus' good enough for dem lady potters wi' dangly earrings wot make coffee mugs wot you can't lift wid both hands. Also, it got a lotta grog in it.'

She looks up.

That's bits of old pots, smashed up really small and mixed in – makes it stronger.

ANGUA: Pottery…but wasn't there an oven at the Dwarf Bread Museum?

CHEERY LITTLEBOTTOM: Yes. But you couldn't use that for baking clay, the size is all wrong. You'd…

ANGUA: You might not get the heat right…? And you said you saw red lights in Father Tubelcek's eyes…. Oh no.

CHEERY LITTLEBOTTOM: What?

ANGUA: Pottery. Glowing eyes…

CHEERY LITTLEBOTTOM: What?

ANGUA: A *Golem*? Come on!

CHEERY LITTLEBOTTOM: Where are we going?

ANGUA: To the slaughterhouse district…we need to speak to a butcher!

CHEERY LITTLEBOTTOM: A butcher…?

They exit as the lights blackout.

SCENE TEN

Back at the front door of the College of Heralds. PARDESSUS enters backwards, ushering out NOBBY NOBBS, who looks totally stunned.

PARDESSUS: Has your lordship got everything he requires?

NOBBY NOBBS: *(Incapable of speech.)* Nfff.

PARDESSUS: If we can be of any help whatsoever –

NOBBY NOBBS: Nnnf.

PARDESSUS: Sorry about your boots, m'lord, but the wyvern's been ill. It'll brush off no trouble when it dries.

NOBBY starts to totter off. PARDESSUS turns to the audience.

He even walks nobly, wouldn't you say? It's disgusting that he's a mere corporal, a man of his breeding.

Blackout.

SCENE ELEVEN

The Watch House. VIMES is on. VISIT enters.

VISIT: Excuse me, Commander Vimes? It's about those words you asked me to check.

COMMANDER VIMES: What words?

VISIT: The ones on that paper in Father Tubelcek's mouth. You said to try and find out what they meant. It's ancient Cenotine, sir. It's out of one of their holy books, although of course when I say 'holy' it is a fact that they were basically misguided in a…

COMMANDER VIMES: Yes, yes, I'm sure. Does it by any chance say 'Mr X did it, aargh, aargh, aargh'?

VISIT: No, sir.

COMMANDER VIMES: Pity.

VISIT: That phrase does not appear anywhere in any known holy book, sir.

COMMANDER VIMES: Of course.

VISIT: And I looked at other documents in the room and the paper does not appear to be in the deceased's handwriting, sir.

COMMANDER VIMES: Ah-ha! Someone else's? Does it say something like 'Take that, you bastard, we've been waiting ages to get you for what you did all those years ago'?

VISIT: *(Wearily.)* No, sir. Although that phrase *does* appear in the Apocrypha to The Vengeful Testament of Offler. However, *these* words are from the Cenotine Book of Truth.

COMMANDER VIMES: And…?

VISIT: These are just some of the rules that their god allegedly gave to the first people after he'd baked them out of the clay, sir. Rules like 'Thou shall labour fruitfully all the days of your life', sir, and 'Thou shalt not kill', and 'Thou shalt be humble'. That sort of thing.

COMMANDER VIMES: Any idea why it was in his mouth?

VISIT: No, sir.

COMMANDER VIMES: *(Unfair.)* A note is left at the scene of a crime in my town and does it have the decency to be a death-threat? No. It's a bit of religious doggerel. What's the good of Clues that are more mysterious than the mystery?

VISIT: Couldn't say sir.

COMMANDER VIMES: No.

Cross fade to ANGUA and CHEERY walking up to a door

ANGUA: You're a watchman, Knock on the door and tell them to open up.

CHEERY LITTLEBOTTOM: Me? They won't take any notice of me!

ANGUA: You're going to have to do it sooner or later. Go on.

CHEERY knocks.

CHEERY LITTLEBOTTOM: City Watch! Open up or we'll have your guts for starters!

ANGUA: Good first effort.

The door opens and MR SOCK enters.

ANGUA: Mr Sock? We'd like to speak to an employee of yours. Mr Dorfl.

GERHARDT SOCK: Mr Dorfl? What's he done now?

ANGUA: We'd just like to talk to him. May we come in?

GERHARDT SOCK: I have a choice?

ANGUA: Let's say – you have a *kind* of choice.

She sniffs, theatrically.

Rat? I didn't know you supplied the dwarf market, Mr Sock.

GERHARDT SOCK: Dorfl! Come here right now!

DORFL enters.

ANGUA: Have you got something to do, Mr Sock?

GERHARDT SOCK: No, I've…

ANGUA: You *have* got something to do, Mr Sock.

GERHARDT SOCK: Ah. Er? Yes. Okay. I'll just go and see to the offal boilers . .

He exits.

CHEERY LITTLEBOTTOM: Is it a troll made to look like a human? Look at those glowing eyes!

ANGUA: It's not a troll. It's a golem. A man of clay. It's… a machine.

She moves over to DORFL.

I'm going to read your chem, Dorfl.

DORFL writes on his slate:

YES

ANGUA opens the golem and removes the chem. The golem slumps.

ANGUA: *(To CHEERY.)* Some kind of holy writing. It always is. Some old dead religion.

CHEERY LITTLEBOTTOM: You've killed it?

ANGUA: No. You can't take away what isn't there.

She puts the scroll back. The golem comes alive.

His 'life' is in those words…the words in his head.

There have been two murders. I'm pretty certain a golem did one and probably both.

CHEERY LITTLEBOTTOM: Sorry, look… Are you telling me this…thing is powered by words?

ANGUA: Why not? Everyone knows words *do* have power. Their life is to work, to obey commands. They never rest. Golems have to work; they have to have a master. They can work underwater, or in total darkness, or knee-deep in poison. For years.

CHEERY LITTLEBOTTOM: But that's slavery!

ANGUA: Of course it isn't. You might as well enslave a doorknob.

She turns back to DORFL.

Do you have time off from working here?

He shakes his head.

But you sometimes leave the slaughterhouse? To make deliveries?

He nods his head.

And meet other golems? Now *listen*, Dorfl, I *know* you keep in touch somehow. And, if a golem is killing *real* people, I wouldn't give a busted teacup for your chances.

The GOLEM shrugs.

Do you know Father Tubelcek?

He nods.

Where were you when he was killed?

He points to the shop.

You were here all time? Twenty-four hours a day?

He nods.

Thank you. You can go back to your work. We know where to find you.

DORFL exits.

CHEERY LITTLEBOTTOM: It was lying.

ANGUA: You're probably right. But the slaughterhouse is a huge place. I bet we wouldn't be able to prove it'd stepped out for half an hour. I think I'll suggest that we put it under special surveillance.

CHEERY LITTLEBOTTOM: What, like…plain clothes?

ANGUA: *(Carefully.)* Something like that.

CHEERY LITTLEBOTTOM: I've got a lot to learn, I can see. I never thought you had to carry bits of garlic, for a start!

ANGUA: It's special equipment if you're dealing with the undead. The sword and truncheon don't work on everyone.

CHEERY LITTLEBOTTOM: Well, I knew about garlic and vampires. And I've got a silver chainmail vest – but is anything else good for werewolves?

ANGUA: A gin and tonic's always welcome.

CHEERY LITTLEBOTTOM: Angua? Why do you wear your badge on a collar round your neck?

ANGUA: Well…so it's always handy. You know. In any circumstances.

CHEERY LITTLEBOTTOM: Do I need to do that?

ANGUA: *(As they exit.)* I shouldn't think so.

MR SOCK enters and watches them leave. DORFL appears behind him, holding out his slate.

GERHARDT SOCK: Dorfl, you damn stupid lump! *Never* sneak up behind a man – I've told you before!

He reads DORLF's slate

TONIGHT I CANNOT WORK. GOLEM HOLY DAY

What? The bacon slicer never asks for time off!

He sighs.

All right. They did mention this when I bought you. I don't know how we're going to manage… Be back quickly, then…

DORLF starts to exit across the stage.

Or I'll –

Weakly.

You be back quickly, d'you hear?

He sighs and exits. Two ROBED FIGURES cross the stage, their backs to the audience, their faces obscured by hoods.

FIRST ROBED FIGURE: At least it's clean this way. And it would be for the good of the city, of course.

SECOND ROBED FIGURE: And he won't die?

FIRST ROBED FIGURE: Apparently he can be kept merely… unwell.

SECOND ROBED FIGURE: Good. I'd rather have him unwell than dead. I wouldn't trust Vetinari to stay in a grave.

FIRST ROBED FIGURE: I heard that he once said he'd prefer to be cremated, as a matter of fact.

SECOND ROBED FIGURE: Then I just hope they scatter the ashes really *widely,* that's all.

FIRST ROBED FIGURE: *(Exiting.)* What about the Watch?

SECOND ROBED FIGURE: *(Exiting.)* What about it?

Blackout.

SCENE TWELVE

The Patrician's Palace. VETINARI is wrapped up on a chair. DOUGHNUT JIMMY is just leaving as VIMES enters.

LORD VETINARI: Ah, Vimes.

COMMANDER VIMES: How are you feeling, sir?

LORD VETINARI: Truly dreadful. Who was that little man?

COMMANDER VIMES: Doughnut Jimmy, sir.

LORD VETINARI: Ah. He gave me milk and some sort of sticky potion. I was heartily sick. Funny phrase, that. *Heartily* sick. Sounds… Rather cheerful.

COMMANDER VIMES: Yes, sir.

LORD VETINARI: Feel like I've got a bad dose of flu. Head not working properly. Why did he still smell of horses?

COMMANDER VIMES: He's a horse doctor, sir. A damn good one.

LORD VETINARI: Ah. I see. Well, well, well. Should hair ache, Vimes?

COMMANDER VIMES: Couldn't say, sir.

He crosses to the window.

Everything all right, Constable Downspout?

DOWNSPOUT: *(Off.)* Eff, fir.

LORD VETINARI: What was that, Vimes?

COMMANDER VIMES: Constable Downspout's a gargoyle, sir. when it conies to staying in one place, sir, you can't beat him. Nothing'll get past him. And I have Watchmen on every landing and stairwell.

LORD VETINARI: Well done, Vimes.

Pause.

And now, don't let me detain you.

COMMANDER VIMES: Wha – ?

LORD VETINARI: If you wouldn't mind. And I'm sure a lot of paperwork has accumulated in my office, so if you'd send someone to fetch it, I would be obliged.

VIMES salutes rather tetchily and turns to exit.

Thank you, Vimes.

LORD VETINARI: *(As he writes.)* 'The tincture of night began to suffuse the soup of the afternoon…'

Tincture. *Tincture.* A distinguished word…pleasantly countered by the flatness of 'soup'. The *soup* of the afternoon. Yes. In which may well be found the croutons of teatime….

He rises, unsteadily, and crosses to the window.

Still there, Constable Downspout?

DOWNSPOUT: *(Off.)* Yeff, fir.

VETINARI returns to his chair.

LORD VETINARI: A gargoyle, eh? Very ingenious, Vimes. I wondered why the Watch has indented for five pigeons a week on its wages bill. A gargoyle in the Watch, whose job it was to watch. Now then…

He turns several pages, each time licking his finger pointedly. Aloud.

'Chapter Eight. The Rites of Man.'

Ah, yes…

He slumps over the desk.

Blackout.

SCENE THIRTEEN

The Watch House. COLON is on, with mug of tea. NOBBY enters, looking dejected and carrying a scroll. He flops into a chair by COLON.

NOBBY NOBBS: It's terrible, Fred. Terrible! I've been elevated, Fred!

SGT COLON: Nasty! Did you see who did it?

NOBBY hands him the scroll.

NOBBY NOBBS: You do your best, you keep your head down, you don't make any trouble, and then something like this happens to you.

SGT COLON: Nobby, you've read this? It says you're a *lord!*

NOBBY NOBBS: Fred, what am I gonna *do*?

SGT COLON: Sit back and eat off ermine plates, I should think!

NOBBY NOBBS: That's just it, Fred. There's no money. No big house. No land. Not a brass farthing!

SGT COLON: I thought all the upper crust had pots of money.

NOBBY NOBBS: Well, I'm the crust on its uppers, Fred. I don't know anything about lording! I don't want to have to wear posh clothes and go to hunt balls and all that stuff.

SGT COLON: Does anyone else know about this?

NOBBY NOBBS: Only Mr Vimes.

SGT COLON: Well, there you are. You don't have to tell anyone. Then you don't *have* to go around wearing golden trousers, and you needn't hunt balls unless you've lost 'em.

NOBBY NOBBS: You're a toff, Fred.

SGT COLON: That makes two of us, m'lord! Get it? Get it?

NOBBY NOBBS: *(Wearily.)* Don't, Fred.

DETRITUS enters, ushering a member of the public out of the Watch House.

CANDLE MAKER: I tell you it's not right. Me! A craftsman! Given the sack! Fifteen years at Spadger and Williams, right, Candlemakers to the nobility. And then they go bust 'cos of Carry undercutting 'em and I get a job at Carry's and, bang, I'm out of a job *there,* too! 'Surplus to requirements'! Bloody golems! Forcing real people out of a job!

DETRITUS: Shame.

CANDLE MAKER: Smash 'em up, that's what I say. So I was wond'rin' if there was any chance of a job with you lot, eh?

DETRITUS: I will mention it to the Commander. What is it you do?

CANDLE MAKER: I'm a Wick-Dipper and End-Teaser.

DETRITUS: *(As he ushers him out.)* I can see that's a useful trade.

NOBBY NOBBS: Wouldn't be so bad if there was a pot of cash. I thought you couldn't be a nob without bein' a rich bugger. Don't make sense, bein' nobby *and* poor.

DETRITUS: What's up with Nobby?

SGT COLON: Keep it to yourself, Detritus, but it's because he's a peer.

DETRITUS: Oh. Is that a fact? I'd better go and get the mop, then.

As DETRITUS exits one way, DORFL walks in. He holds up his slate to COLON, who reads:

SGT COLON: *(Reading.)* '*I HAVE COME TO YOU. I GIVE MYSELF UP FOR MURDER. I KILLED THE OLD PRIEST*'

I'd better tell Captain Carrot. You keep it covered, Nobby. Make sure it don't run off.

NOBBY NOBBS: *(As COLON starts to leave.)* Why's *it* going to run off?

COLON exits.

SGT COLON: *(Off.)* Captain…?

Pause.

NOBBY NOBBS: Now – don't you try any funny stuff…right…?

COLON re-enters with CARROT.

SGT COLON: We wrestled a confession out of it.

DORLF holds up his slate. CARROT reads: I AM GUILTY

Something drops from DORFL's hands. CARROT picks it up.

CARROT: A piece of matchstick, by the look of it.

SGT COLON: Mr Vimes is going to be really pleased with us!

CARROT: *(To DORFL.)* Did you kill Father Tubelcek?

DORFL nods.

Why did you do it?

No reply.

And Mr Hopkinson at the Bread Museum?

DORFL nods.

You beat him to death with an iron bar?

DORFL nods.

CARROT moves in close to DORFL. He twiddles the matchstick between his fingers.

I know you didn't kill Mr Hopkinson and I don't think you killed Father Tubelcek. I think he was dying when you found him. I think you tried to save him, Dorfl. In fact, I'm pretty sure I can prove it if I can see your chem –

He opens DORFL's head and removes the paper. DORLF slumps.

CARROT compares DORFL's chem. To the one from FATHER TUBELCEK's mouth.

Look at these, Fred.

SGT COLON: Well…they looks the same.

CARROT: Yes. Letter for letter the same. I think Dorfl wrote these words and put them in old Tubelcek's mouth after the poor man died.

NOBBY NOBBS: That's *mucky,* that is…

CARROT: No, you don't understand. He wrote them because they were the only ones he knew that worked. A bit like the golem kiss of life. A golem knows only one thing that keeps you alive – It's the words in your head. I'll put these back and then I think we'll put a tail on him.

Blackout.

SCENE FOURTEEN

The Watch House. CARROT is on stage, at attention. VIMES is sat, reading a report.

COMMANDER VIMES: *(Looking up.)* Right Captain. Very complete.

CARROT: White clay. It was white clay we found. And practically unbaked. Dorfl's made of dark terracotta, and rock-hard.

COMMANDER VIMES: The last thing the old priest saw was a golem.

CARROT: Dorfl, I'm sure. But Dorfl isn't the murderer.

COMMANDER VIMES: You hear lots of stories about them doing stupid things like making a thousand teapots or digging a hole five miles deep.

CARROT: Yes, but that's not exactly criminal activity, is it, sir? That's just ordinary rebellion.

COMMANDER VIMES: Rebellion?

CARROT: Dumbly obeying orders, sir. Can't be blamed for obeying orders, sir. No one told them how many teapots to make. No one wants them to think, so they get their own back by *not* thinking.

COMMANDER VIMES: They rebel by *working?*

Now listen, we've got a confession and the eyeball evidence. If you can't come up with anything better than a…a feeling, then we'll have to –

CARROT: Have to what, sir? With his chem removed, there *isn't* anything more we could do to him. But I think he knows who killed the priest, sir.

COMMANDER VIMES: Where's Angua gone?

CARROT: She's been following Dorfl sir. I was…puzzled about this, sir.

He holds up the match.

It was in his hand. Golems don't smoke and they don't use fire, sir. It's just…odd.

COMMANDER VIMES: *(Sarcastically.)* Oh good. A Clue.

ANGUA enters.

CARROT: Angua? Where did he go?

ANGUA: I followed him to a cellar in the slaughterhouse district. There were lots of golems there. They were in there for nearly an hour.

CARROT: Doing what?

ANGUA: I went into the cellar after they'd left. The walls were covered with writing:…it was all criss-crossed over itself; different hands. I couldn't make out much… I guess in golem terms it was an argument – using the walls as a big slate. A golem argument. In writing. It got pretty heated, I think. If they were human, they'd have been shouting…

There were these, on the floor.

She holds out ten short broken matches.

COMMANDER VIMES: A golem argument. *(He holds up DORFL's longer match.)* And Dorfl lost.

ANGUA: Er…there was something else, sir. It was a…feeling. Like…deep grief, sir. Terrible, terrible sadness.

CHEERY enters.

COMMANDER VIMES: I need a drink. Pity I don't drink any more eh?

ANGUA: No, sir.

COMMANDER VIMES: No. You're right.

ANGUA: Maybe supper, sir. And some coffee?

COMMANDER VIMES: Yes. Yes, Cheery?

CHEERY LITTLEBOTTOM: I found arsenic, sir. The sample was full of it. But…

COMMANDER VIMES: Well? What was it in?

CHEERY LITTLEBOTTOM: That's just it, sir. It wasn't in anything from the palace. It was the stuff from under Father Tubelcek's fingernails, sir.

COMMANDER VIMES: *What?*

CHEERY LITTLEBOTTOM: There was grease under his nails, sir, and I thought maybe it could've come from whoever attacked him. He might have scratched the murderer?

There's more, sir.

COMMANDER VIMES: Go on.

CHEERY LITTLEBOTTOM: And I had a careful look at the clay we found at the murder scene. You know we knew it had fragments in it of old pottery? Well... I chipped a bit off Dorfl to compare and I think there's some clay just like his in there.

COMMANDER VIMES: One drink could make this all so clear.

CARROT: *(Warning.)* Sir...

COMMANDER VIMES: Don't worry. I know. Any of you know what any of this means?

The others shake their heads.

CARROT: It's been a long day for all of us, sir.

COMMANDER VIMES: Okay. Tomorrow... I want you, Carrot, to check on the golems in the city. If they're up to something I want to know what it is. And you, Littlebottom...you look *everywhere* in the old man's house for more arsenic. Off you go – get some rest.

Blackout.

SCENE FIFTEEN

A street. Dark and misty. ANGUA and CHEERY stroll on.

CHEERY LITTLEBOTTOM: Aren't you afraid – walking alone in these dark streets?

ANGUA: Nope.

CHEERY LITTLEBOTTOM: But I imagine muggers and cut-throats would be out in a fog like this. And you said you lived in the Shades.

ANGUA: Oh, yes. But I haven't been bothered lately.

CHEERY LITTLEBOTTOM: Ah, perhaps they're frightened of the uniform?

ANGUA: Possibly.

CHEERY LITTLEBOTTOM: Er…excuse me…but are you and Captain Carrot…?

ANGUA: Oh, yes, We're *er*. But I stay at Mrs Cake's boarding house because you need your own space in a city like this.

CHEERY LITTLEBOTTOM: I'm staying with my Uncle Armstrangler. It's very boring. People talk about mining most of the time. There must be more interesting things. Hair. Clothes.

ANGUA looks. CHEERY shrugs.

Girl talk. There's no help for it, I'll have to move out. I feel all…wrong.

ANGUA: We're going quite close to Elm Street. Just, er, drop in for a while. I've got some stuff you could borrow…

Lights black as they saunter off.

SCENE SIXTEEN

Patrician's Palace. LORD VETINARI is on, looking poorly. VISIT & DETRITUS are standing beside him. As VIMES enters, VISIT crosses to him.

VISIT: It's Lord Vetinari, sir! It's worse this time!

COMMANDER VIMES: Has anyone sent for Doughnut Jimmy?

VISIT: Yessir! I poked my head in as soon as I came on shift and he was out like a light, sir! Just flaked out on his desk.

COMMANDER VIMES: Who opened the window?

VISIT: I did, sir. Soon as I found him. He looked as though he needed some fresh air.

COMMANDER VIMES: This is Ankh-Morpork, constable. It'd be fresher if you left the window *shut*. Okay, I want everyone, I mean everyone, who was in this place overnight rounded up and in here in two minutes. And someone fetch Corporal Littlebottom. And tell Captain Carrot.

VISIT exits. He looks around the room, at VETINARI's desk. He checks the pen, picks up the inkwell and sniffs it. He picks up VETINARI's journal and reads a bit, licking his finger to turn the page. Then he sniffs his fingers and wipes them on his tunic.

He checks the desk, then picks up a drawing, apparently done by VETINARI.

Did you see this?

DETRITUS: Yes, sir. It looks like a person made up of hundreds of smaller figures. Looks a bit like one of them Wicker Men, but with a crown.

COMMANDER VIMES: Very strange. I suppose his mind was wandering.

He checks the walls.

Where do you stop looking? Splinters in the floor? Blowpipes through the keyhole?
Vetinari was on the mend yesterday. And now he looks worse. Someone got to him in the night. How? Slow poison's a bugger. You have to find a way of giving it to the victim every day.

DETRITUS: Sir?

COMMANDER VIMES: No, you *don't*... You find a way of getting him to administer it to himself every day.

DETRITUS: A poisoned nail, sir?

COMMANDER VIMES: No. Because he wouldn't keep nicking himself. Not every day. *What does he do every day*?

DETRITUS: He writes in his journal, sir.

COMMANDER VIMES: Yes.

He looks at the journal, licking his finger to turn the page.

Can you poison paper? Could he take it that way? Can you breathe arsenic? Cheery said a king in Quirm was killed by poisoned wallpaper, but we've moved him to different rooms…

To DETRITUS.

Are all his rooms decorated with this gloomy green wallpaper?

DETRITUS: Yes, sir.

CHEERY enters.

VIMES: Ah, Cheery. It's not good.

CHEERY LITTLEBOTTOM: I'll mix up some of Mr Doughnut's jollop right away, sir. The staff are outside, sir.

COMMANDER VIMES: Get someone to move him into a different bedroom. Without green wallpaper. Take a sample of it and check it for arsenic. Get the servants to prepare a new room, right?

CHEERY LITTLEBOTTOM: Yes, sir.

COMMANDER VIMES: And, after they've done it, pick a *different* room at random and move him into it. And change *everything*, understand? Every stick of furniture, every vase, every rug –

Are you wearing ear-rings, Littlebottom?

CHEERY LITTLEBOTTOM: Er…yes, sir. Constable Angua gave them to me.

COMMANDER VIMES: Right. OK, then. Right. Good. Well. Off you go then – and send in the night staff.

CHEERY exits and the staff enter. DETRITUS crosses to them.

DETRITUS: I know you all done it. If the person wot done it does not own up der whole staff will be locked up in der Tanty.

He points at a maid.

It was you wot done it, own up!

MAID: No.

DETRITUS: Where was you last night?

MAID: In bed, of course!

DETRITUS: Aha, dat a likely story, own up, dat where you always is at night?

MAID: Of course.

DETRITUS: Aha, own up, you got witnesses?

MAID: Sauce!

COMMANDER VIMES: All right, all right. Thank you, Sergeant. That will be all for now.

Are all the staff here?

MAID: Mildred Easy hasn't been seen since yesterday. She's the upstairs maid. A boy come with a message. She had to go off to see her family.

COMMANDER VIMES: Thank you. OK, you can all go and get on with whatever it is you do. Ah… Mr Drumknott?

The staff exit.

DRUMKNOTT: Yes, Commander?

COMMANDER VIMES: What's this book? Is it his lordship's diary?

DRUMKNOTT: Yes, Commander.

COMMANDER VIMES: He writes in code. Have you been able to crack it?

DRUMKNOTT: *(Taking the book and looking at it.)* I didn't know it was *in* code, Commander.

COMMANDER VIMES: You do know his last secretary tried to kill him?

DRUMKNOTT: *(Opening the book.)* Yes, sir. However, *I didn't* do it.

He delicately licks his finger and turns a page.

VIMES stares at him.

COMMANDER VIMES: All right, thank you.

DRUMKNOTT exits.

COMMANDER VIMES: Detritus, find out where this Mildred Easy lives and nip round there, will you. I'd like to know why she wasn't in work today.

Blackout.

SCENE SEVENTEEN

The Watch House. CARROT is sat at a desk with ANGUA stood by him. Another person – PREBBLE SKINK, is also standing by the desk.

CARROT: Thank you for helping us, sir. We are just trying to get an accurate record of all the golems in the city.
I understand you have one working for you at the sawmill?

PREBBLE SKINK: Had. Sawed his own head off last night.

He pulls a golem head out of a bag.

ANGUA: Oh dear, another one.

PREBBLE SKINK: It was weird. Sidney said it went on sawing all the way up to the moment it sawed its head right off. 'Ere… Alf told me he heard in the Drum last night that golems have been murderin' people.

CARROT: Enquiries are continuing. Did your golem leave the yard yesterday evening?

PREBBLE SKINK: Well, yeah, early on… Something about a holy day. You got to let them go, otherwise the words in their heads –

CARROT: And then it came back and worked all night?

ANGUA: Sawing pine logs?

PREBBLE SKINK: Yes, that's right. *(He pulls a slate out of the bag.)* This was on his slate.

CARROT: *(Reading.)* 'Thou Shall Not Kill' 'Clay of My Clay. Ashamed.' Do you have any idea why it'd write that?

PREBBLE SKINK: Search me. Hey, perhaps it went potty? Get it? Clay…pot…potty ?

CARROT: Thank you. We will keep these as evidence. Good morning.

SKINK exits.

Why did you ask about pine logs?

ANGUA: I smelled the same pine resin in the cellar. This golem was in there.

CARROT: They *all* were. And now they're committing suicide.

We hear VIMES' voice as he and CHEERY storm in.

COMMANDER VIMES: What do you mean, 'nothing'? It's got to be the book! He licks his fingers to turn a page, and every day he gets a little dose of arsenic! Fiendishly clever!

CHEERY LITTLEBOTTOM: Sorry, sir. I can't find a trace.

COMMANDER VIMES: Damn! For half an hour there I really thought I'd got it…

CHEERY LITTLEBOTTOM: Oddly, though, sir, we have found traces in some rats served in the local dwarf delicatessen, sir. Quite a few reports of food poisoning. Let me put it like this – if those rats had been poisoned with lead instead of arsenic, you'd have been able to sharpen their noses and use them as pencils.

COMMANDER VIMES: Poisoned rats? How would they get access to arsenic? We're missing something here. If you want to poison someone slowly you've either got to give them small doses all the time – or, at least, every day. We've covered everything the Patrician does. It can't be the air in the room. We've been in there every day.

DETRITUS enters.

DETRITUS: Scuse me, sir. I went round to der address of dat maid called Easy like you said. Dere was cryin' women all round der door. An' I remember what you said about dat dipplo word –

COMMANDER VIMES: Diplomacy.

DETRITUS: Yeah. Not shoutin' at people an' dat. I fought, dis look a delicate situation. So I fought I'd better leave it to you, sir.

COMMANDER VIMES: Thank you, Sergeant. Corporal Littlebottom, with me. *(As they exit.)* Er… Littlebottom?

CHEERY LITTLEBOTTOM: Sir?

COMMANDER VIMES: Is that…?

CHEERY LITTLEBOTTOM: Lipstick, sir. Yes. Constable Angua gave it to me, sir.

COMMANDER VIMES: Lipstick. Yes. Well. That was kind of her.

And lights blackout as they exit.

ACT TWO

SCENE ONE

The Rats Chamber. A meeting of the Guild Heads. ROSIE PALM (Seamstresses), MR BOGGIS (Thieves), MR SLANT (Lawyers), MR CARRY (Candlemakers), LORD DOWNEY (Assassins), QUEEN MOLLY (Beggars), GERHARDT SOCK (Butchers) and others.

ROSIE PALM: Quiet, please! Gentlemen! Ladies!

Dr Downey?

LORD DOWNEY: My friends, I think we are all aware of the situation –

QUEEN MOLLY: Yeah, so's your accountant!

Nervous laughter.

LORD DOWNEY: I can assure you once again, gentlemen – and ladies – that I am aware of no contract with us regarding Lord Vetinari. In any case, I cannot imagine that an Assassin would use poison in this case. His lordship spent some time at the Assassins' school. No doubt he will recover.

ROSIE PALM: And if he doesn't?

LORD DOWNEY: No one lives forever. Then, no doubt, we would get a new ruler.

GERHARDT SOCK: Thing is…the thing is…it's been…you've got to admit it…it's been OK…well, think about some of the others…at least Vetinari isn't actually insane.

ROSIE PALM: Under Vetinari it has certainly been safer to walk the streets –

GERHARDT SOCK: You should know, madam.

A few sniggers.

ROSIE PALM: *I meant* that a modest payment to the Thieves' Guild is all that is required for perfect safety.

MR CARRY: And, indeed, a man may visit a broth – a house of ill –

ROSIE PALM: Negotiable affection.

MR CARRY: Indeed, and be quite confident of not waking up stripped stark naked and beaten black and blue.

ROSIE PALM: Unless his tastes run that way.

SLANT: Life has certainly been more reliable under Vetinari.

BOGGIS: He *does* have all street-theatre players and mime artists thrown into the scorpion pit.

SLANT: True. But he has his bad points too.

BOGGIS: Fair point. But do you remember all those fights? All the little gangs of thieves fighting all the time? It got so that there was hardly any energy left to actually steal things.

SLANT: Things are indeed more…reliable now. Whatever else you might say about Lord Vetinari, he does make sure today is always followed by tomorrow.

ROSIE PALM: I am only a weak woman. But it does seem to me that there's an opportunity here. Either there's a long struggle to sort out a successor, or we sort it out now. Yes?

GERHARDT SOCK: But who'd want it? You get the power, but you get the problems, too. You have to negotiate and juggle with all the conflicting interests. No one sane had tried to kill Vetinari for *years,* because the world with him *in* it was just preferable to one *without* him.

MR CARRY: It's all more complicated now. And power goes to people's heads.

QUEEN MOLLY: And then other people's heads fall off, Mr Carry!

SLANT: Speaking as the President of the Guild of Lawyers. I must recommend stability in this matter. Stability…equals monarchy.

Minor uproar.

Look at Klatch. Generations of Seriphs. Result: political stability. Oh, monarchs come and go, they depose one another, and so on and so forth, but the *institution* goes on.

LORD DOWNEY: And where does this king come from, may I ask?

SLANT: There have been precedents. Monarchies who have found themselves bereft of a convenient monarch have… obtained one.

BOGGIS: Sorry? Are you saying we *send out* for a king?

SLANT: Certainly. And one who will be…amenable.

ROSIE PALM: I like the sound of that.

MR CARRY: Hear, hear.

SLANT: And a suitable person exists. Here in this city. Within the City Watch…

Pause.

He is Corporal C. W. St J. Nobbs.

QUEEN MOLLY: Nobby Nobbs? You're talking about *Nobby Nobbs?*

SLANT: He is the last known descendant of the Earl of Ankh, who could trace *his* descent all the way to a distant cousin of the last king.

LORD DOWNEY: Small monkey-like chap, Spotty?

QUEEN MOLLY: That's Nobby!

LORD DOWNEY: Him? But the man's a tit!

MR CARRY: And dim as a penny candle. But – malleable, perhaps? Blood *will* out.

ROSIE PALM: When I've watched him go down the street I've always thought: 'There's a man who walks in greatness.'

BOGGIS: And he squeezes his spots in a very regal way. Very graciously.

MRS PALM: I must remind you that poor Lord Vetinari is still alive.

SLANT: Indeed. And long may he remain so. I've merely set out for you one option against that day, may it be a long time coming, when we should consider a…successor.

QUEEN MOLLY: What about Vimes?

LORD DOWNEY: He is a servant of the city. Surely *we* represent the city?

QUEEN MOLLY: Hah! He won't see it that way. And you know what Vimes thinks about kings. It was a Vimes who chopped the head off the last one. He won't like it. That's all I tell you. Vetinari keeps Vimes wound up. No knowing what happens if he unwinds all at once –

LORD DOWNEY: Nevertheless. There's a soiree at Lady Selachii's house this evening. I believe Nobbs is being invited. Perhaps we can…meet him.

Blackout.

SCENE TWO

Cockbill Street. VIMES is on, talking to a girl (MILDRED EASY) and a man in a doorway; both have black armbands. CARROT stands respectfully to one side. VIMES thanks the two, who return into their home. He crosses to CARROT.

COMMANDER VIMES: What have we missed, Captain?

CARROT: Sir?

COMMANDER VIMES: In his lordship's bedroom. There's the bed. The desk. Things on the desk. The table by the bed. The chair. The rug. Everything. We replaced everything. He eats food. We've checked the food, yes?

CARROT: The whole larder, sir.

COMMANDER VIMES: Really? We might be wrong there. I don't understand how, but we might be wrong. *(Angry.)* There are two people…an old lady and a *child*…lying in the cemetery that suggests we are wrong.

What else is there? Littlebottom says there's no marks on him. What else *is* there? Let's find out the *how* and with any luck that'll give us the *who*.

CARROT: He breathes the air in his room more than anyone else, si –

COMMANDER VIMES: But we moved him into another bedroom! Even if someone was, I don't know, pumping poison in…they couldn't change rooms with us all watching. It's got to be the food!

CARROT: I've watched them taste it, sir.

COMMANDER VIMES: And then?

CARROT: It goes on the dumb waiter up to his Lordship's room, sir.

COMMANDER VIMES: Then it's something we're not seeing, damn it! People are *dead,* Captain! Mrs Easy's *dead!*

CARROT: Sir?

COMMANDER VIMES: She just brought up nine kids in a couple of rooms you couldn't stretch out in and she sewed shirts for tuppence an hour, every hour the bloody gods sent, and all she did was work and keep herself to herself and she is *dead,* Captain. And so's her grandson. Aged fourteen months. Because her granddaughter took them some grub from the palace! A bit of a treat for them! And d'you know what? Mildred thought I was going to arrest her for theft!

It's *murder* now. Not assassination, not politics, it's *murder.*

Have we checked the salt?

CARROT: Sir?

COMMANDER VIMES: Salt! Mustard! Vinegar! Pepper! We didn't check all the food and then let his lordship tip poison on to suit his taste, did we? Arsenic's a metal. Can't you get…metal salts? Tell me we asked ourselves that. We aren't that stupid, are we?

CARROT: I'll check directly.

COMMANDER VIMES: Not yet. The spoon. What's it made of?

CARROT: Good point. I'll check the cutlery, too, sir.

COMMANDER VIMES: Now we're cooking with charcoal! So… we've got the tray and you put the tray in the dumbwaiter and then what?

CARROT: The men in the kitchen haul on the ropes and it goes up to the sixth floor.

COMMANDER VIMES: No stops? It goes up six floors. I'll bet there's a door into it on every floor. Our poisoner just stands there, bold as you like, and waits for the tray to come by, right?

CARROT: Brilliant, sir!

COMMANDER VIMES: It happens at night, I'll swear. He's chipper in the evenings and out like a light next morning. What time is his supper sent up?

CARROT: Around six o'clock, sir, when he's poorly. It's got dark by then. Then he gets on with his writing.

COMMANDER VIMES: Right. We've got a lot to do. Come on.

A moment. COLON crosses the stage and knocks at another door. A woman answers.

SGT COLON: Oh, good afternoon, madam. Sorry to bother you. I expect it's your busy time, but I've got to ask, just to eliminate you from our enquiries, so to speak. Do you use any arsenic around the place?

MR CARRY: *(Off.)* Don't leave the officer standing there, Fanley. Bring him in. At once.

He appears in the door.

Good afternoon, officer. How may we help you?

SGT COLON: Checking up on arsenic, sir. Seems some's been getting where it shouldn't.

MR CARRY: Er…good heavens. Really. I'm sure we don't use any, but do come inside while I check with the foremen. I'm certain there's a pot of tea hot, too.

COLON enters. A moment, and then the door bangs shut, followed by the turning of a heavy key and some bolts, with a very terminal, prison-cell sort of sound to them.

Blackout.

SCENE THREE

Patrician's Palace. LORD VETINARI is sat up, as before. DRUMKNOTT stands by him. It is around sunset and orange light illuminates the room as the scene starts. VIMES enters.

LORD VETINARI: Ah, Vimes.

COMMANDER VIMES: Your supper will be up shortly, my lord. I have arranged for an officer to travel up in the dumb waiter with it and to nail shut all the doors on the way up.

Rattling, off, of the dumb waiter.

LORD VETINARI: Very thorough, Vimes.

COMMANDER VIMES: And can I once again say that our job would be a lot easier if you let us move you out of the palace?

LORD VETINARI: I'm sure it would be.

CHEERY enters, with a pizza on a plate, on a tray.

COMMANDER VIMES: Any problems, Cheery?

CHEERY LITTLEBOTTOM: Very dull all the way up, sir. There were other doors and they all looked pretty unused, but I nailed 'em up anyway like you said, sir.

COMMANDER VIMES: Well done. Down you go.

CHEERY gives the tray to VIMES and exits. Noise of dumb waiter descending. The sunlight is now darkening into night.

LORD VETINARI: Every detail covered, eh, Vimes?

COMMANDER VIMES: I hope so, sir.

He passes the tray to VETINARI.

LORD VETINARI: What's this?

COMMANDER VIMES: A Klatchian Hots without anchovies.
We got it from Ron's Pizza Hovel round the corner.
The way I see it, no one can poison all the food in the city.
And the cutlery's from my place.

LORD VETINARI: You have the mind of a true policeman, Vimes.

He looks at the pizza.

Has someone already eaten this, Vimes?

COMMANDER VIMES: No, sir. That's just how they chop up
the food.

LORD VETINARI: Oh, I *see.* I thought perhaps the food-tasters
were getting over-enthusiastic. *(With heavy irony.)* My word.
What a treat I have to look forward to.

COMMANDER VIMES: I can see you're feeling better, sir.

LORD VETINARI: Thank you, Vimes.

VIMES salutes and exits.

DRUMKNOTT: I will leave you to it, my Lord. It's getting dark,
sir – shall I light the candles?

LORD VETINARI: Yes. Thank you, Drumknott.

Thank goodness for Vimes, eh Drumknott?

DRUMKNOTT: *(Lighting the candles on VETINARI's table.)* Indeed,
my Lord.

LORD VETINARI: There is something quite endearing about
his desperate, burning and above all *misplaced* competence.

DRUMKNOTT: Yes, my Lord.

LORD VETINARI: *(With a sigh.)* Really. If the poor man takes
any longer about it, I shall have to start giving him hints.

DRUMKNOTT: Indeed, sir.

He starts to leave.

Remember, sir, that you are not yet well. Please do not
work too late, sir.

He exits as the lights fade on VETINARI, *reaching past his pizza to turn a page of his journal.*

SCENE FOUR

The Watch house. CARROT *is on with* DORFL. *He has just put* DORFL's *chem back, and* DORFL *is reactivating.*

CARROT: Tell me about the golem who killed people.

No reaction.

The others have killed themselves.

DORFL nods.

CARROT: *How* do you know?

You feel what other golems feel?

DORFL nods.

And people are killing golems all over the city. Smashing them up because they think you're all killers. I think I know what's happening, Dorfl. Some of it. Clay of your clay. Shaming you all. Something went wrong. You tried to put it right. I think…you all had such hopes.

No reaction.

You sold him, didn't you. Why? Is it because golems must have a master?

No reaction from DORFL.

CARROT: I'm wondering if the old priest and Mr Hopkinson did something…or *helped* to do something. I'm wondering if…afterwards…that something turned against them, found the world a bit too much for it.

No reaction.

You're free to go. What happens now is up to you. I know you've all got a secret. But, the way things are going, there won't be any of you left to keep it.

No reaction from DORFL.

57

Well, I won't force you. Although, you know, I could. I could write a few extra words on your chem. Tell you to be talkative.

DORFL turns to face him.

But I won't. Because that would be inhumane. Go on. You can go. It's not as if I don't know where you live.

DORFL exits.

Dash it.

ANGUA & CHEERY enter.

I've sent Dorfl home. But it's probably not a good time for a golem to be out alone so I'm just going to stroll along after him and keep… Are you all right, Corporal Littlebottom?

CHEERY LITTLEBOTTOM: Yes, sir.

CARROT: You're wearing a skir….…..a…a…a kilt?

CHEERY LITTLEBOTTOM: Yes, sir.

ANGUA: I'll come with you. Cheri can keep an eye on the desk.

CHEERY exits back into the Watch House. CARROT and ANGUA stroll.

CARROT: Do you think there's something a bit… *odd* about Littlebottom?

ANGUA: Seems like a perfectly ordinary female to me.

CARROT: *Female?* He *told* you he was female?

ANGUA: She. This is Ankh-Morpork, you know. I know you're a dwarf by adoption, Carrot, but we do have extra pronouns here.

CARROT: Well, I would have thought she'd have the decency to keep it to herself. I mean, I've nothing against females. I'm pretty certain my stepmother is one. But I don't think it's very clever, you know, to go around drawing attention to the fact.

ANGUA: Carrot, I think you've got something wrong with your head.

CARROT: What?

ANGUA: I think you may have got it stuck up your bum.

Come on – he went this way.

They exit as the lights blackout.

SCENE FIVE

LADY SELACHI's Mansion. Cocktail party in progress. On stage are as many people as you can manage. NOBBY enters and is stopped by the FOOTMAN.

FOOTMAN: Servants' entrance.

NOBBY NOBBS: Read these.

FOOTMAN: *(Reading.)* I, after hearing evidence from a number of experts, including Mrs Slipdry the midwife, certify that the balance of probability is that the bearer of this document, C. W. St John Nobbs, is a human being. Signed, Lord Vetinari.

NOBBY NOBBS: And the invitation.

FOOTMAN: Oh, I am terribly sorry, your lordship. Please, do go in.

He announces.

The Earl of Ankh, Corporal the Rt. Hon. Lord C. W. St J Nobbs!

Conversation stops. Heads turn.

LORD VENTURI: But the man's an absolute oik –

The FOOTMAN moves over to NOBBY.

FOOTMAN: A drink, m'lord?

NOBBY NOBBS: Thanks. I'll have a pint of Winkle's.

LADY SELACHI: Winkles?

FOOTMAN: A type of beer, ma'am.

He exits to fetch it.

NOBBY NOBBS: 'Ere – have you heard the one about the Klatchian who walked into a pub with a tiny piano –

The FOOTMAN re-enters with the beer, which he delivers to NOBBY and then announces.

FOOTMAN: The buffet is ready, m'lady.

NOBBY NOBBS: Got any pig knuckles? Goes down a treat with Winkles, a plate of pig knuckles.

Never tried a pig knuckle? You just can't beat it.

He raises his glass.

Up the hatch! Here's looking at your bottom!

As he swigs, and starts to talk to two adjacent guests, LORD VENTURI leans in to LADY SELACHI.

LORD VENTURI: Good humoured little tit, in his way.

Give him his pint of beer and he seems as happy as a pig in muck.

LADY SELACHI: I think that's somewhat insulting. I've known some splendid pigs.

Do you think he can read?

LORD VENTURI: Does it matter?

LADY SELACHI: Can you see any princess marrying him?

LORD VENTURI: Dragon King of Arms did well with his lineage stuff. I suppose the little tit isn't *really* an earl, by any chance?

LADY SELACHI: Don't be silly.

NOBBY has finished his beer, and we hear him just finishing off a joke.

NOBBY NOBBS: And the butler says – 'No, we never found his head'!

NOBBY laughs. The others join in, feebly. LADY SELACHI and VENTURI cross to him.

LORD VENTURI: Ah, Lord de Nobbes.

NOBBY NOBBS: Wotcha.

LORD VENTURI: Could we have a word?

We were just talking, my lord, about the future governance of the city now that poor Lord Vetinari's health is so bad…

LADY SELACHI: It would obviously upset the current equilibrium if we looked for a new Patrician at this point. Besides, are any of the guild leaders up to the task? I think not. Perhaps it is time for the monarchy to reveal itself…?

NOBBY NOBBS: Not to worry, then. Everyone knows we've got a king hanging around. No problem there. Send for Captain Carrot, that's my advice.

LORD VENTURI: Ah, yes. Captain Carrot. But is he the right man? I know he has a sword and a birthmark, but we would need a king from a lineage that is *used* to command.

LADY SELACHI: Like *yours*, my lord.

NOBBY NOBBS: King? King? And have Mr Vimes cut me head off?

LORD VENTURI: What?

NOBBY NOBBS: Mr Vimes'd go spare! He'd go *spare*!

LADY SELACHI: When you're *king*, my Lord, you can tell that wretched Sir Samuel what to do. You'll be, as you would call it, 'the boss'.

NOBBY NOBBS: Tell Vimesey what to do?

LADY SELACHI: That's right!

NOBBY NOBBS: He'd go *spare*!!!

LORD VENTURI: Listen, you silly little man –

LADY SELACHI: – Lord –

LORD VENTURI: You silly little lord, you'd be able to have him executed if you wished!

61

NOBBY NOBBS: I couldn't do that!

LORD VENTURI: Why not?

NOBBY NOBBS: He'd go spare! I can't be king! Ole Vimes'd go spare!

LORD VENTURI: *Will you stop saying that!*

NOBBY NOBBS: 'S a bit hot in here. Which way's the door?

LADY SELACHI: Over there –

NOBBY is already legging it, a fast as his little legs can carry him.

Cross-fade to VIMES' bedroom. Night. VIMES sits writing by candlelight. Wind noise outside.

COMMANDER VIMES: *(His voice, over the speakers.)* Right. What have we got? 'Arsenic'

He writes that and circles it.

'Grease under Tubelcek's fingernails'

He writes that and circles it

'Golems'

He writes that and circles it.

(Aloud.) Why would a golem admit to something it hadn't done?

What did Mr Hopkinson have that anyone would want? Dwarf bread? Nah. Oven…? Hm.

(Over the speakers again.) There was arsenic under the old priest's fingernails. And poisoned rats have been turning up in the city's diners. Maybe he'd put poison down for them?

Hang on – Oven. Hopkinson had an oven…what if the golems decided to make themselves…a golem?

Gods, I could do with a drink!

(Aloud.) No I couldn't. Best thing I ever did, swearing off the booze.

He moves his foot and there is a chink.

What the –

He reaches down and pulls up a bottle of whisky.

(Over the speakers.) How the hell did that get here. Not rotgut neither – finest single malt.

So – someone's playing silly buggers, eh?

He uncorks it and smells the contents as the lights cross-fade to a street. Windy night. Cloaked and hooded, MR CARRY scuttles across the stage. He reaches a doorway and sidles in. DRAGON KING OF ARMS appears.

MR CARRY: I have one of the Watch locked up. I had to. He was getting too close!

DRAGON KING OF ARMS: You got me here for *this*? There's a *werewolf* in the Watch! Ah-ha. Not one of your freaks. She's a proper bimorphic! If you tossed a coin, she could smell what side it came down!

It will take her no time at all to find him!

MR CARRY: How about if we kill him and drag his body away?

DRAGON KING OF ARMS: You think she couldn't smell the difference between a corpse and a living body?

Idiot. Why couldn't you have let him look around? What could he have seen? I know that copper. Sgt Colon? Stupid man. Let him go, but send Meshugah after him.

MR CARRY: Are you sure? It's getting *odd*. It wanders off and screams in the night, and they're *not* supposed to do that. And it's cracking up. Trust dumb golems not to make it properly!

I heard that Vimes is –

DRAGON KING OF ARMS: I've seen to Vimes!

Now get rid of that Watchman before they find him on your premises! Quickly!

He slopes off. CARRY hurries off separately.

SCENE SIX

Watch Office. CARROT, ANGUA and DORFL enter to a desk. MR SOCK enters and stands by the desk. A candle burns on the desk.

CARROT: Thank you for coming to see us, Mr Sock. We are returning your golem. He was on his way to see you and we had to rescue him. Some townspeople tried to smash him.

GERHARDT SOCK: Are you mad? You think I want *that* back?

CARROT: He's your property.

GERHARDT SOCK: Haven't you heard the stories? I'm not having one of those under my roof!

CARROT: If you don't take him back, I'll have to charge you with littering. Cluttering the street with unwanted pottery.

GERHARDT SOCK: Oh, be serious!

CARROT: I always am.

ANGUA: He always is.

GERHARDT SOCK: I don't want a killer working in my slaughterhouse! You have it, if you're so keen!

CARROT: Are you trying to bribe an officer of the law, Mr Sock?

GERHARDT SOCK: Are you insane?

CARROT: I am always sane.

ANGUA: *(With a sigh.)* He always is.

CARROT: Watchmen are not allowed to accept gifts. But I *will* buy him from you. For a fair price.

GERHARDT SOCK: Well, that's different. It was worth $530 when I bought it, but of course it's got additional skills now –

ANGUA: You were prepared to give it away a moment ago!

CARROT: I'll pay you a dollar.

GERHARDT SOCK: A dollar? That's daylight robb –

ANGUA: *(Grabbing his neck.)* It's *night-time!*

GERHARDT SOCK: A dollar. Right. A fair price. One dollar.

CARROT: *(Paying him.)* A receipt is very important. A proper legal transfer of ownership.

GERHARDT SOCK: *(Scribbling on a scrap of paper.)* Right. Right. Right. Happy to oblige.

CARROT: Thank you very much, Mr Sock.

MR SOCK exits.

ANGUA: Oh, well done. So now you own a golem.

CARROT: Dorfl? Here's your receipt. You don't *have* to have a master. That means you belong to you.

No reaction.

I don't think he understands. It's quite hard to get some ideas into people's heads...of course.

He opens DORFL's head and pops in the receipt. DORFL reacts.

DORFL: Thsssss....

DORFL turns and stalks off, quickly. MRS PALM, MR BOGGIS & LORD DOWNEY enter.

ROSIE PALM: Ah – Captain Carrot!

CARROT: Mrs Palm? And Lord Downy... Mr Boggis...? What can I –

LORD DOWNEY: Captain Carrot, we are here to discuss this terrible matter of the poisoning of Lord Vetinari.

CARROT: You really ought to talk to Commander Vimes –

LORD DOWNEY: I believe that on a number of occasions Commander Vimes has made derogatory comments to you about Lord Vetinari...?

CARROT: You mean like 'He ought to be hung except they can't find a twisty enough rope'?

65

LORD DOWNEY: And I believe he personally took over the investigation of the poisoning?

CARROT: Well, yes. But –

LORD DOWNEY: Didn't you think that was odd?

CARROT: No, sir. I think he's got a sort of soft spot for the Patrician, in his way. He once said that if anyone was going to kill Vetinari he'd like it to be him.

LORD DOWNEY: Indeed? And I understand that his efforts to discover the poisoner have not reached any conclusions?

We would like to inspect the Commander's office.

CARROT: I don't know if that's –

LORD DOWNEY: Think very carefully. We three represent most of the guilds of this city. You will of course accompany us to see that we do nothing illegal. We feel we have a good reason for inspecting the Commander's office.

VIMES strides angrily in, carrying an empty bottle of whisky and a paper packet.

COMMANDER VIMES: Looking for what? This perhaps? *(He holds up the whisky.)* Or this? *(He holds up the packet.)*

I found these – *planted* in my desk drawer. Anyone here know who by?

BOGGIS: We had information…

COMMANDER VIMES: Oh, you had information, did you Boggis? You hear that, Captain? They had information. So that's all right!

BOGGIS: We were acting in good faith.

COMMANDER VIMES: Let me see… Your information was something on the lines of: Vimes is dead drunk in the Watch House and he's got a bag of arsenic in his desk? And I'll just bet you wanted to act in good faith, eh?

ROSIE PALM: You are correct, Sir Samuel. We were all sent a note.

She pulls a note out of her bag and hands it to VIMES.

And I can see we have been misinformed...

She glares at BOGGIS and DOWNEY.

Do allow me to apologize. Come, gentlemen.

They exit.

COMMANDER VIMES: Not a brick dislodged or a tile loose outside my office window – and the front office had been manned all day. Odd, that. How could anyone get in?

ANGUA: Could've flown in, sir.

COMMANDER VIMES: Hm.

He looks at the note.

And I shouldn't think we'll be able to find any clues on this. There's too many greasy fingermarks all over it.

When we find the man responsible...somewhere at the top of the charge sheet is going to be Forcing Commander Vimes to Tip a Whole Bottle of Single Malt on to the Carpet. That's a hanging offence.

CARROT: It's disgusting! Fancy them even thinking that you'd poison the Patrician!

COMMANDER VIMES: I'm offended that they think I'd be daft enough to keep the poison in my desk drawer.

I was expected to go 'At last, alcohol!', and chugalug the lot without thinking. Then some respectable pillars of the community were going to find me, in your presence, too – which was a nice touch – with the evidence of my crime neatly hidden but not so well hidden that they couldn't find it.

He hands over the arsenic packet to ANGUA.

Get Littlebottom to have a look at this.

ANGUA exits. He puts the whisky bottle on the desk and turns to CARROT.

You know, I feel quite perked up. The old brain has begun to work at last. You know the golem that did the killing?

CARROT: Yes, sir?

COMMANDER VIMES: Do you know what was *special* about it?

CARROT: The golems made it themselves, I think. But of course they needed a priest for the words and they had to borrow Mr Hopkinson's bread oven.

And it's gone mad, sir. I mean they drove it mad, sir. The other golems. They didn't mean to, but it was built-in, sir. They wanted it to do so many things. It was like their… child, I think. All their hopes and dreams. And when they found out it'd been killing people…well, that's *terrible* to a golem.

CHEERY enters with the packet.

CHEERY LITTLEBOTTOM: You wanted me to look at this powder, Commander? It could be arsenous acid, sir. I'll have to test it, of course.

COMMANDER VIMES: Arsenic. As I thought. Er…what's that on your hands?

CHEERY LITTLEBOTTOM: Nail varnish, sir.

COMMANDER VIMES: Er…fine, fine. Funny, I thought it would be green.

CHEERY LITTLEBOTTOM: Not really my colour, sir.

COMMANDER VIMES: I meant the arsenic, Littlebottom.

CHEERY LITTLEBOTTOM: Oh, you can get all sorts of colours of arsenic, sir. And you can cook them up with nitre and you get arsenous acid, sir. You have to use a well ventilated room, sir. Nasty fumes.

COMMANDER VIMES: Dangerous stuff.

CHEERY LITTLEBOTTOM: Not good at all, sir. But useful. Tanners, dyers, painters… It's not just poisoners that've got a use for arsenic.

COMMANDER VIMES: I'm surprised people aren't dropping dead of it all the time.

CHEERY LITTLEBOTTOM: Oh, most of them use golems, sir –

A pause.

CARROT: These golems. They'd be *covered* in arsenic, would they?

CHEERY LITTLEBOTTOM: Could be, sir.

COMMANDER VIMES: Grease under his fingernails. The old priest scratched at his murderer. Grease under his fingernails. With arsenic in it.

It's there, Captain. Something we haven't seen.

CARROT: But we've looked everywhere.

COMMANDER VIMES: So we've seen the answer and haven't seen that it is the answer. And if we don't see it now, at this moment, we'll never see it at all…

Something we don't see. Something invisible. No! Something we don't see because it's always there. Something that strikes in the night…

The penny drops.

My gods. I've got it!

CARROT: What, sir?

COMMANDER VIMES: 'There it is,' he said softly. There. On my desk. You see it?

CARROT: What, sir?

COMMANDER VIMES: The thing that's poisoning his lordship. There it is…on the desk. See?

CHEERY LITTLEBOTTOM: He drinks Bearhugger's whisky?

CARROT: The blotter? Poisoned pens?

COMMANDER VIMES: Hah! I didn't ask Mildred Easy what else she took! But of course they're a servant's little bonus, too! And old Mrs Easy was a seamstress, a *proper* seamstress! And this is autumn! Killed by the nights drawing in! See?

CARROT: *(Looking at the desk.)* No, sir.

COMMANDER VIMES: Of course you can't. Because there's nothing to see. You can't see it. That's how you can tell it's there. If it wasn't there you'd soon see it! Only you wouldn't! See?

What is it I'm always telling you?

CARROT: Er… Never trust anybody, sir?

COMMANDER VIMES: No, not that.

CARROT: Everyone's guilty of something, sir?

COMMANDER VIMES: Not that, either.

CARROT: Er…er… Just because someone's a member of an ethnic minority doesn't mean they're not a nasty small-minded little jerk, sir?

COMMANDER VIMES: N– When did I say that?

CARROT: Last week, sir.

Er…What *have* we found, sir?

COMMANDER VIMES: You'll see! We're going to the palace. Fetch Angua. We might need her. And bring the search warrant. And Sergeant Colon, too.

CHEERY LITTLEBOTTOM: He hasn't signed in again yet, sir. He should have gone off-duty an hour ago.

COMMANDER VIMES: He'll be staying out of trouble somewhere. Get the lads to find him. Come on!

They exit as the lights blackout.

SCENE SEVEN

The Palace. Palace staff enter – MILDRED EASY and a couple of others at least. As the lights come up, VIMES, CARROT, ANGUA and CHEERY are being 'escorted' in by DRUMKNOTT.

DRUMKNOTT: Commander…was there something…?

COMMANDER VIMES: Is Mildred Easy here?'

MILDRED steps forward.

It's all right, Mildred. I just need to ask you a few more questions –

MILDRED EASY: I'm…s-s-sorry, sir –

COMMANDER VIMES: You haven't done anything wrong. But you didn't just take food home for your family, did you?

What else did you take?

MILDRED EASY: There was the old sheets but Mrs Dipplock did *say* I could have – oh, and some boot polish…

COMMANDER VIMES: No, not those. Look…*everyone* takes small things from the place where they work. Small stuff that no one notices. No one thinks of it as stealing. Odds and ends, Miss Easy? I'm thinking about the word 'ends'.

MILDRED EASY: Er…you mean…the candle ends, sir?

COMMANDER VIMES: *Yes!* You take home the candle stubs? I expect you get the ones from the bedrooms, yes?

MILDRED EASY: Yessir. They're much better than the ole coarse ones we use in the main halls, sir.

DRUMKNOTT: We get ours from Carry's in the Shambles, sir. *Very* reasonable prices. We used to deal with Spadger and Williams but Mr Carry's really cornered the market these days, hasn't he?

COMMANDER VIMES: And you put these candles in his lordship's room every day? And nowhere else? And you take your, er, perks…the candle ends…home?

And I expect your Gran sat up with your little brother, did she? Because I expect he got took sick first, so she sat up with him all night long, night after night and, hah, if I know old Mrs Easy, she did her sewing by candlelight.

MILDRED EASY: That's right, sir.

CHEERY LITTLEBOTTOM: The wicks are full of arsenous acid, sir? Well done, sir!

ANGUA: What an evil way to kill anyone.

COMMANDER VIMES: Certainly very clever. Vetinari sits up half the night writing, and in the morning the candle's burned down. Poisoned by the light. The light's something you don't see. Who looks at the light? Not some plodding old copper.

CARROT: *(Cheerfully.)* Oh, you're not that old, sir.

Quickly – seeing VIMES' look.

Or that plodding, either.

COMMANDER VIMES: We didn't look at the light because the light is what we look *with*. Okay. And now I think we should go and have a look at the candle factory. Carrot? Angua? Take Cheery and get down to Carry's tallow works. Just keep an eye on things and wait for me.

FRED COLON staggers in.

Fred? Where've you been?

SGT COLON: Sir, I was tied up and shoved in a cellar and heroically broke free, sir! And I was chased by one of them golems, sir!

COMMANDER VIMES: Where was this?

SGT COLON: It was a place in the Shambles. Candlemakers. They tied me up with wick string, sir.

COMMANDER VIMES: Well done, Fred. That's corroboration.

Now. Let's try policing like grandfather used to do it. It's time to –

CARROT: Prod buttock, sir?

COMMANDER VIMES: Close.

Blackout.

SCENE EIGHT

The Candleworks. CARROT, CHEERY and ANGUA enter just as the KING GOLEM crosses the stage and enters the plant.

CARROT: I was right, they did make themselves a golem. A King Golem. They thought a king would make them free.

CHEERY LITTLEBOTTOM: But you can't bake pottery in an old bread oven!

ANGUA: Commander Vimes told us to wait for him.

CARROT: Yes, but we don't know what might be going on in there. We can't just hang around.

Aside to ANGUA.

I wish Mr Vimes hadn't wanted us to bring her. Supposing something happens to her?

ANGUA: What are you talking about?

CARROT: Well…you know…she's a girl.

ANGUA: So what? *I'm* a girl!

CHEERY LITTLEBOTTOM: I can hear, you know!

ANGUA: *(Sniffing.)* There's been a vampire here…

CARROT: I think we'd –

CARRY bursts in, with a crossbow.

ARTHUR CARRY: I knew you'd find out! I wish I'd never bought the damned thing! I've got a bow! I warn you, I've got a crossbow!

CARROT: Ah, Mr Carry. Captain Carrot, City Watch –

ARTHUR CARRY: I know who you are! I know who you are! And *what* you are, too! I knew you'd come!

ANGUA: *What* we are?

ARTHUR CARRY: I didn't even want to get involved! It killed those old men, didn't it?

CARROT: Yes.

ARTHUR CARRY: Why?

CARROT: Because they helped make it, I think. It knew who to blame.

ARTHUR CARRY: The golems sold it to me! I thought it'd help build up the business but the damned thing won't stop –

I've had to lay off everyone except the girls in the packing department, and *they're* on three shifts and overtime! I've got four men out looking for tallow, two negotiating for wicks and three trying to buy more storage space!

CARROT: Then get it to stop making candles. All you have to do is change the words in its head.

ARTHUR CARRY: It won't let me! Don't you think I've tried?

CARROT: What about the poisoned candles?

ARTHUR CARRY: That wasn't my idea! This has all gone far too far… I'm getting out.

CARROT: Whose idea was it, Mr Carry?

ARTHUR CARRY: Oh no! I'm not going to end up in some alley somewhere with as much blood as a banana!

ANGUA: Who's the vampire?

ARTHUR CARRY: I never said anything about him! He said we could get the golem to do anything…

CARROT: Like making poisoned candles?

ARTHUR CARRY: Yes, but he said it'd just keep Vetinari out of the way. And he's not dead, 'cos I'd have heard. I shouldn't think making him ill is a crime, so you can't –

CARROT: The candles killed two other people. An old lady and a baby in Cockbill Street.

ARTHUR CARRY: Were they important?

CARROT: I was almost feeling sorry for you. Right up to that point. You're a lucky man, Mr Carry. We got to you before Commander Vimes did. Now, just put down the crossbow and we can talk about –

ANGUA steps towards CARRY.

ARTHUR CARRY: Careful… *Corporal* – the arrow point is silver…not good for your species.

The KING GOLEM enters. CARRY runs off.

CARROT: Maybe we can reason with it –

ANGUA: Attention! This is the *real* world calling!

CARROT: You have the right to a lawyer…

ANGUA: Carrot…?

DORFL enters and starts to fight with the KING GOLEM. They bash at each other, then gradually move off stage, still fighting. GOLEM crashes continue off.

CARROT: We ought to help him!

ANGUA: How? If *he* can't stop it, what can *we* do..??

Huge crash, off. VIMES rushes on.

COMMANDER VIMES: What's happening? Angua?

ANGUA: They're killing each other!

Explosion, off. Bits of golem fly on – from the KING GOLEM and from DORFL. CARROT rushes off. A moment, and he returns with DORFL's head.

CARROT: *(Solemnly.)* We can rebuild him. We have the pottery.

COMMANDER VIMES: Do it. Right now. And when you rebuild him. Give him a *voice.* Understand?

CARROT: Yes, sir.

CARROT and ANGUA exit to the 'body'. CARRY sneaks on behind VIMES and CHEERY, trying to escape. He carries the crossbow and a heraldic shield. He is almost off when VIMES sees him.

COMMANDER VIMES: Oi!

ARTHUR CARRY: Stay back – I have a crossbow!

COMMANDER VIMES: Just give yourself up.

ARTHUR CARRY: No. I have to get away. My life's worth nothing in this city.

He backs towards an alley.

COMMANDER VIMES: That won't help you, Carry. That's a dead end.

CARRY exits. Scream, off. CHEERY rushes off. A moment. CHEERY returns, carrying the shield.

Dead?

CHEERY LITTLEBOTTOM: Dead, sir. But how, sir? It's a dead end. No other way out.

COMMANDER VIMES: Unless you can fly.

He takes the shield from CHEERY.

Look at this. This is what is was about for Carry. Respectability. His own coat of arms. And a huge clue.

CHEERY LITTLEBOTTOM: Sir?

COMMANDER VIMES: It's full of heraldic clues – at the top here…a fish-shaped lamp – because Carry's ancestors were fishmongers supposedly – but in heraldry they'd call it a 'lampe au poisson'…sounds a bit like a lamp of poison…? And the rest of the design looks a lot like the shield of the Guild of Assassins – another oh-so-funny heraldic clue.

CHEERY LITTLEBOTTOM: Dragon King of Arms, sir?

COMMANDER VIMES: Dragon King of Arms, Corporal. Just as soon as we've rebuilt Dorfl.

Blackout.

SCENE NINE

College of Heralds. VIMES enters, carrying a crossbow. Then DRAGON KING OF ARMS confronts him.

DRAGON KING OF ARMS: Commander Vimes. To what do I owe the pleasure?

COMMANDER VIMES: Pleasure's all mine, sir. I'm here to arrest you. Might I point out the arrow, sir? Made of wood, sir. Not metal. Like a wooden stake, you might say.

DRAGON KING OF ARMS: Thoughtful. You still haven't told me of what I am accused.

COMMANDER VIMES: Complicity in the murders of Mrs Flora Easy and the child William Easy. Murder of Arthur Carry. Attempted murder of Lord Vetinari…though personally I'd call that mitigating circumstances.

DRAGON KING OF ARMS: You really intend to prefer charges?

COMMANDER VIMES: I'd *prefer* violence. Charges is what I'm settling for.

DRAGON KING OF ARMS: You have no evidence.

COMMANDER VIMES: My officers have the testimony of the late Arthur Carry. And only someone who could fly could have killed him, and got undetected into my office to plant the poison and that whisky bottle.

DRAGON KING OF ARMS: I really have no idea…

COMMANDER VIMES: You treat people like cattle. Your heralds even keep their stock records here. I bet you've had a lot of influence over people's bloodlines over the centuries.

DRAGON KING OF ARMS: A little.

COMMANDER VIMES: Is Nobby really an earl?

DRAGON KING OF ARMS: The evidence suggests so.

COMMANDER VIMES: Yes, but that's *your* evidence, isn't it. You cook the books. I don't think Nobby's noble. I don't believe in that ring. That doesn't make him Earl of Ankh.

The amount of stuff his family's nicked over the years you could prove he was the Dowager Duchess of Quirm. He stole my cigar case once and I'm damn sure he isn't me. Nobby's no nob. He was just convenient. Someone you could control.

I mean – Carrot was your obvious candidate but, hell, he really is honest and fair and just and that was no good at all.

The rumours all said the king was a common watchman, and they don't come any more common than Nobby.

But people didn't want to kill Vetinari. That would make things happen too fast. You had to gently remove him while you got everyone to buy into your new commoner king.

DRAGON KING OF ARMS: Very interesting Vimes, but –

COMMANDER VIMES: So you bribed Carry to make poisoned candles. Using his new golem.

DRAGON KING OF ARMS: You seem keen to involve me. But Carry was only another customer…

COMMANDER VIMES: You made up his damn coat of arms! You made sure it looked like the Assassins' shield! You put in the poison/lamp joke! The grey metal cord – for the arsenic-soaked wick – and the oh-so funny motto. 'Art Brought Forth the Candle'? Why in modern language, eh? They're usually in Latatian. And in Latatian, I am reliably told, it would read 'Ars Enixa est Candelam'. 'Ars Enixa' 'Arsenic'. Ho Ho Ho. Arsenic is the Candle…how you must have laughed.

You *showed* me that coat of arms when I came here.

So – Carry got a coat of arms and respect. What did you get?

Control. That's what.

It's all got messy under Vetinari. The wrong sort of people are rising to the top.

DRAGON KING OF ARMS: You have no evidence, Vimes.
And that crossbow can't hurt me – not at night, not out of
my coffin.

*He moves to VIMES, grabs the crossbow and clutches VIMES around
the neck.*

COMMANDER VIMES: No, sir. Not normally. But if you'd been
weakened. By inhaling, say, essence of holy water.

Dragon looks at the candles.

Soak the wicks in holy water. The water evaporates,
leaving just holiness…

DRAGON KING OF ARMS: That's not possible!

Trying to trick me into an admission, Vimes?

COMMANDER VIMES: Oh, I had that when you looked at the
candles, sir.

DRAGON KING OF ARMS: Really? But who else saw me?
Only you.

DORFL enters.

DORFL: I Saw.

DRAGON KING OF ARMS: You gave him a voice?

DORFL: *(Grabbing DRAGON KING OF ARMS.)* Yes. I Could
Kill You. This Is An Option Available To Me As A Free-
Thinking Individual But I Will Not Do So.

COMMANDER VIMES: Take him away, Dorfl. Put him in the
Palace Dungeons.

DORFL: *(As he leaves with DRAGON.)* Undead or Alive, You Are
Coming With Me.

Blackout.

79

SCENE TEN

The Patrician's Palace. VIMES & DRUMKNOTT, waiting. A moment, then VETINARI (completely fit and well) sweeps on.

LORD VETINARI: Ah, Vimes. It seems to have been a very busy night last night…

COMMANDER VIMES: Yes, sir.

LORD VETINARI: It appears that I have Dragon King of Arms in the cells.

COMMANDER VIMES: Yes, sir.

LORD VETINARI: I've read your report. Somewhat tenuous evidence, I feel.

COMMANDER VIMES: Sir?

LORD VETINARI: One of your witnesses isn't even alive, Vimes.

COMMANDER VIMES: No, sir. Neither is the suspect, sir. Technically.

LORD VETINARI: It also appears I have to commend you, Commander.

COMMANDER VIMES: Sir?

LORD VETINARI: The Heralds at the Royal College of Arms, or at least at what remains of the Royal College of Arms, have sent me a note saying how bravely you worked last night. To rescue all their animals from the unfortunate fire which seems to have destroyed their building…

COMMANDER VIMES: Sir?

LORD VETINARI: … Along with the provenances of many splendid old families. Of course, the Heralds will do what they can, and the families themselves keep records but frankly, I understand, it's all going to be patchwork and guesswork. Extremely embarrassing. Are you smiling, Commander?

COMMANDER VIMES: Trick of the light, sir.

Anyone told Dragon King of Arms, sir?

LORD VETINARI: He screamed a lot, Vimes, I am told. And I gather he uttered a number of threats against you, for some reason.

COMMANDER VIMES: I shall try to fit him into my busy schedule, sir.

LORD VETINARI: It seems I've only got to be unwell for a few days and you manage to upset everyone of any importance in this city.

In all I've had seventeen demands for your badge. Some want parts of your body attached. Why did you have to upset everybody?

COMMANDER VIMES: I suppose it's a knack, sir.

LORD VETINARI: Workshop owners, assassins, priests, butchers…you seem to have infuriated most of the leading figures in the city. Really, it seems I have no choice. As of this week, I'm giving you a pay rise.

COMMANDER VIMES: Sir?

LORD VETINARI: Nothing unseemly. Ten dollars a month.

Tell me, Sir Samuel, do you know the phrase 'Quis custodiet ipsos custodes?'?

COMMANDER VIMES: Something about trifle, is it?

LORD VETINARI: It means 'Who guards the guards themselves?'.

Who watches the Watch? I wonder?

COMMANDER VIMES: Oh, that's easy, sir. We watch one another.

LORD VETINARI: Really? An intriguing point… However, in order to keep the peace, the golem will have to be destroyed.

COMMANDER VIMES: No, sir.

LORD VETINARI: I'm sure I just gave you an order, Commander. I distinctly felt my lips move.

COMMANDER VIMES: No, sir. He's alive, sir.

LORD VETINARI: He's just made of clay, Vimes.

COMMANDER VIMES: Aren't we all, sir?

LORD VETINARI: I've had no less than nine missives from leading religious figures declaring that he is an abomination.

COMMANDER VIMES: Yes, sir. I've given that viewpoint a lot of thought, sir, and reached the following conclusion: arseholes to the lot of 'em, sir.

LORD VETINARI: *(With a carefully concealed smile.)* Sir Samuel, you are a harsh negotiator. Surely you can give and take?

COMMANDER VIMES: Couldn't say, sir.

LORD VETINARI: What will you use the golem for?

COMMANDER VIMES: Not *use,* sir. Employ. I thought he might be useful for to keep the peace, sir.

LORD VETINARI: A watchman?

COMMANDER VIMES: Yes, sir. Haven't you heard, sir? Golems do all the mucky jobs.

He salutes, very smartly, and marches out.

LORD VETINARI: He does so like a dramatic exit.

DRUMKNOTT: Yes, my lord.

LORD VETINARI: *(Pulling a length of candle from his robe.)* Dispose of this somewhere safely, will you? It's the candle from the other night.

DRUMKNOTT: It's not burned down, my lord? But I saw the candle end in the holder…

LORD VETINARI: Oh, of course I cut off enough to make a stub and let the wick burn for a moment. I couldn't let our gallant policeman know I'd worked it out for myself, could I? Not when he was making such an effort and having so much fun being…well, being *Vimes.* I'm not *completely* heartless, you know.

DRUMKNOTT: But, my lord, you could have sorted it out diplomatically! Instead he went around upsetting things and making a lot of people very angry and afraid – Ah.

LORD VETINARI: Quite so.

DRUMKNOTT: May I make an observation, my lord?

The thought occurs, sir, that if Commander Vimes did not exist you would have had to invent him.

LORD VETINARI: You know, Drumknott, I rather think I *did*.

Blackout.

SCENE ELEVEN

The Watch House. ANGUA *enters, carrying a large bag.* CHEERY *comes to her.*

CHEERY LITTLEBOTTOM: You don't have to go, you know.

ANGUA: Yes, I do. I don't know if I can take the Watch seriously and…and sometimes I think Carrot's working up to ask me…and, well, it'd never work out. It's the way he just *assumes* everything, you know? So best to go now.

CHEERY LITTLEBOTTOM: Won't Carrot try to stop you?

ANGUA: Yes, but there's nothing he can say.

CHEERY LITTLEBOTTOM: He'll be upset.

ANGUA: Yes. And then he'll get over it.

She hands CHEERY *the bag.*

Do you want these dresses? I've never got round to wearing them. I expect you could cut them down.

CHEERY LITTLEBOTTOM: Urn . . .

ANGUA: Yes?

CHEERY LITTLEBOTTOM: Er… You've never actually *eaten* anyone, have you?

ANGUA: No.

CHEERY LITTLEBOTTOM: I mean, I only *heard* my second cousin was eaten by werewolves. He was called Sfen.

ANGUA: Can't say I recall the name.

CHEERY LITTLEBOTTOM: That's all right, then.

But I didn't think you'd –

ANGUA: Look, don't get the wrong idea. It's not a case of not wanting to. It's a case of wanting to and *not doing it.*

CHEERY LITTLEBOTTOM: Hrolf Thighbiter's asked me out. And I'm almost *certain* he's male!

CARROT enters.

Er, shall I go away?

ANGUA: Too late…

CARROT: Ah, good morning, Corporal Miss Little-bottom! Hello, Angua. I was just coming to see you. Er . . .

ANGUA: I know what you're going to ask.

CARROT: You do?

ANGUA: I know you've been thinking about it. You knew I was wondering about going.

CARROT: It was obvious, was it?

ANGUA: And the answer's no. I wish it could be yes.

CARROT: It never occurred to me that you'd say no. I mean, why should you?

ANGUA: Good grief, you amaze me. You really do.

CARROT: I thought it'd be something you'd want to do. Oh, well…it doesn't matter, really.

ANGUA: It doesn't *matter?*

CARROT: I mean, yes, it'd have been nice, but I won't lose any sleep over it.

ANGUA: You won't?

CARROT: Well, no. Obviously not. You've got other things you want to do. That's fine. I just thought you might enjoy it. I'll do it by myself.

ANGUA: What? How can…?

What are you *talking* about, Carrot?

CARROT: The Dwarf Bread Museum. I promised Mr Hopkinson's sister that I'd tidy it up. I don't mind giving up a few days off. I just thought it might cheer you up, but I appreciate that bread isn't everyone's cup of tea.

ANGUA: Yes. Right.

CARROT: I'll leave you to it, then.

He strolls off. A pause.

CHEERY LITTLEBOTTOM: Want the dresses back?

ANGUA: Maybe one or two.

THE END